Encyclopedia of
American Oak
Furniture

Robert W. & Harriett Swedberg

Published by

krause
publications

700 E. State Street • Iola, WI 54990-0001
Telephone: 715/445-2214

Please, call or write us for our free catalog of antiques and collectibles publications. To place an
order or receive our free catalog, call 800-258-0929. For editorial comment and further information,
use our regular business telephone at (715) 445-2214

Library of Congress Catalog Number: 00-104620
ISBN: 0-87341-877-8

Printed in the United States of America

Dedication

We dedicate this book to the hundreds of friends we have made while antiquing and writing in both the United States and abroad.

Table of Contents

Acknowledgements

Ackerman's Newton Road Antiques
Bill & Karen Ackerman
Iowa City, Iowa

Bob & Karen Adams

Bob Anderson

Louise Anderson & Larry Crowder

Ruth Ankrom & Linda Cron

Antique America
Cheryle, Lance, and Norman Frye
Davenport, Iowa

Antique and Specialty Center
Colleen Higgins & Stephen Bunton
Anchorage, Alaska

Antique Corner in the Yapp
Building
Wayne & Audrey Yapp
Mt. Horeb, Wisconsin
Antique Mall

Antiques in the Olde White Church
Jim & Judy Ball
Hills, Iowa

Antiques Mall of Madison
Madison, Wisconsin

Antiques Unlimited

Douglas & Marie Blair
Murfreesboro, Tennessee

Randy Bahnsen

Banowetz Antiques
Virl & Kathy Banowetz
Maquoketa, Iowa

Mildred M. Bark

Andy & Pat Baysingar

Sue & Randy Beecham

Bill & Dot Best

Bloomington Antique Mall
Doug & Beverly Jennings
Bloomington, Illinois

Stephen & Carol Bond

Dennis & Laura Brennan
The Brenner Collection

David & Edna Brown

Denise Brown

Vickie Bruss Harter

Buttermilk Hill Antiques
Terry & Evangeline Husk
Franklin, Pennsylvania

Bill & Gwen Carter

Ronnie Carter

Cats & Dogs Antiques
John & Norma Beecher
West Branch, Iowa

Mr. & Mrs. Ralph O. Clark

Columbus Antique Mall & Museum
Norm & Virginia Hageman
Columbus, Wisconsin

Edward Conradt

Kathleen Constable

The Coopers
Jane & Florence
Marion, Iowa

Cottage Antiques
Janet Goetz

The Antique Mall
Iowa City, Iowa

Country Charm Antiques

Dan & Sandy Kitts
Lacon, Illinois

Country Corners, Ltd.
Jerry & Jeanne Plagge
Latimer, Iowa

Ralph Crafton

William Crawford

Kathy Culligan

Pat, Hoss, & Denise Davie

Tom Dawson

Russ & Judy Day

Bob. M. DeBerry

Rev. & Mrs. Kenneth Douglas

Tommy L. Douglas & Richard
E. Kruger

Allen Edwards & Loren Randle

Marlene & Dick Faust

Ann Figg

Gloria & Gale Flynn

Forgotten Treasures
Cheryl & Terry Walker
Rockford, Illinois

Madge Foulk

Foxy's Antiques
E. Lenore "Foxy" Hawpe
Denver, Colorado

Bev Froelinger

Mr. & Mrs. Edward Gabrys

Garland's Antiques
Garland Miller at Rocky's
Antique Mall
Weyer's Cave, Virginia

Martha & Wilbur Gibson

The Glass Case
Grace Jochimsen
The Antique Mall
Iowa City, Iowa

Grandma's Trunk

Audrey Miller

Grand River Merchants
George & Gloria VanDusen
Williamston, Michigan

Philip Gregory

Bob & Mary Grueskin

Gary E. Hale

Lida M. Hale

Mel & Terri Hall

Steve & Virgina Hallett

Mr. & Mrs. Byron Hansen

Dee & Bernard Harding

Ron, Nancy, Shane, & Seth Harness

Arlene Harrington

Arnold & Shirley Hawk

Nina & Chip Heffren

Rhea Heppner

Marjorie Herman

Charles W. Hilliard

Estelle Holloway

Dale & Teresa Hoffman

Lamont and Lillian Hultgren

Carole Hyer

Illinois Antique Center
Dan & Kim Philips
Peoria, Illinois

J. & S. Antiques & Antiques Mall
Jim & Sandy Boender
Manlius, Illinois

Jeffrey's Antique Gallery
Bryan J. Krick
Findlay, Ohio

Virgina Jensen

Shirley Jessen

6 •

Craig & Eric Johnson

Rosemary & Howard Johnson

Elease Jones

Kalona Antique Company
Ken & Brenda Herington
Kalona, Iowa

Nancy Kennedy

Ken's Antiques & Collectibles
Kenneth Kite at Rocky's
Antiques Mall
Weyers Cave, Virginia

Shirley Kilgard

Richard and Bernice King

Dolores & Daniel Kirkham

Marc & Mona Klarman

Chuck & Cindy Kleckner

Clarissa O. Koehn

Leslee & Duane LaMere

Rose Lang

Laub's Loft
Myron & Marge Laub
Nepsonset, Illinois

Darlene & Walter Laud

Laura Renee Antique &
Collectibles

Ben, Ellie, & Laura Goossen

Antique Emporium
Arvada, Colorado

Richard Lee

Marlene Lehr

Richard Lentz & Vivian
Brezezinski

Mary Levery

Mary Little

Sharon Lord

Louisville Antique Mall
Louisville, Kentucky

Linda Lusk

Gary & Lorraine Lynch

Evelyn Maxwell

Joan. W. McCall

Sam & Lawanna McClure

Mr. & Mrs. James L. McDaniel

W.D. McDonald
Columbia Antique Mall
Columbia, South Carolina

Mrs. Rosalie Mehall

Melon City Antique Mart
Joe & Mary Cline
Muscatine, Iowa

Mike's Antiques

Arvada Antique Emporium II
Arvada, Colorado

Keith & Shirley Miller

Miska's Antique Workshop
Rocky's Antique Mall
Weyers Cave, Virginia

Howard Moore

L. E. Morin

Linda & Jeffrey Moyer

Dale & Jennie Rylander

Mike & Sharon Naylor

Old Village Antiques
Joyce L. Ingram
Williamston, Michigan

Richard & Pat Olson

Sharon & Dick Olson

Patricia Hayes Antiques
Bittersweet Shop
Gaylordsville, Connecticut

Ron & Adrienne Petersen

Brad, Jan, Ryan & Sara Pierce

Larry & Gloria Pratt

Plaza Antique Mall
Patricia Zwyghuizen
Grand Rapids, Michigan

Pleasant Hill Antique Mall &
Tea Room
Bob & Eileen Johnson
East Peoria, Illinois

Poor Richard's Antiques
Richard & Karen Melton
Spooner, Wisconsin

Terry, Gretchen, & Andy
Poffinbarger

Jim & Fawna Radewan

Clark & Carolyn Reed

Barb & Fred Rhoades

Walt & Esther Rickertsen

Chuck & Dee Robinson

Earle & Betty Robison

Deb & Randy Robison

Rocky's Antique Mall
Rocky Simonetti
Weyers Cave, Virginia

Ginger Roper

Anne Ross

Mary & Ski Rozanski

School Days Mall
Judy & Eric Sewell
Sturtevant, Wisconsin

Pat & Wynn Scott

Gisela Schroeder

Don & Helen Schwenneker

Charlie & Helen Shaffer

Sharron's Antiques
Steve & Sharron
Hartford, Wisconsin

Gary Shriver

Mr. & Mrs. C. A. Siegfried, Jr.

Rick Shunick

Norval & Nedra Smith

Tom & Vicki Sneddon

Joseph & Gen Sonneville

Everett Sorenson

Warren K. Sparks

Don & Alice Strube

Cheryl Swedberg

Phil Taylor Antiques
Ottumwa, Iowa

Fred & Diane Thomas

Tim Thompson & Gordon Bloomer

John & Denise Van Berkum

Victorian House Antiques
Wayne & Bertha Hoffman
Moline, Illinois

Vintage Books & Clothing

Joe & Pam Michaud
The Antique Mall
Iowa City, Iowa

Pat & Mike Voss

Denny & Judy Waddell

Shirley & Syd Waggoner

Karen, Cody & Adam Watson

Nanette Wayer

Webb's Antique Mall
Verlon Webb
Centerville, Indiana

Shirley & Marvin Williams

Introduction

Oak has long been used as a furniture wood. Jacobean furniture, characterized by twisted turnings and ornamental carvings, was prevalent in England circa 1603-1688. This style experienced a revival around the 1870s in the United States. After America's virgin walnut forest began to be depleted, light-in-color oak became the predominant furniture wood. Since oak trees grew prolifically on the North American continent, they were readily available to lumber companies. Since then, oak has consistently been one of the main furniture woods.

While black walnut is consistently dark in appearance, oak is more versatile. Oak is naturally light-colored in appearance but can be treated to take on different tones. There are various finishes found on oak from the late 1800s and early 1900s. When orange shellac was applied, often with pigments added, the result was called "golden oak." This finish was often described in advertisements as "highly polished" or with a "high-gloss golden finish."

Oak can be fancy or plain. Golden oak furniture often features pressed or carved designs. Frequently these designs are fashioned independently and applied to a piece. Turnings, pillars, grotesque figures, paw or claw feet, incised carvings and other embellishments adorn bedroom sets, dining room pieces, parlor chairs and hall furnishings among others. Mission furniture, on the other hand, is stoic and plain with strong, simple lines. Mission pieces often have distinctive large hardware, obvious mortise and tenon joinings and unadorned wooden uprights. Both the plain mission and the fancy golden oak furnishings were much sought in the homes of the early 1900s – as they are still sought today.

Many factors contribute to the popularity of oak furniture and accessories. Oak furniture continues to be readily available at antique shops, estate sales and auctions. Many young people have an affectionate and nostalgic feeling towards oak furniture as it reminds them of their grandparent's furniture. Many oak pieces such as beds and dressers can still function in modern homes as they did in late 19th and early 20th century homes. Other pieces, such as wardrobes and file cabinets, can be adapted for new purposes acting as entertainment centers or as storage units for videotapes and compact discs.

Unique designs appeal to those who decorate with oak furniture. The use of carved or applied decorations ranges from the simple spoon carving to intricately carved lions' heads that serve as the base of a table (see page 58). Two designs often used for decoration are grotesques and gargoyles. Because of their size they are most often found on large pieces of oak furniture such as sideboards, wardrobes, combination bookcase-desks and china buffets.

Currently, oak furniture with its golden glow is selling well in antique shops. Prices presented in this book are to be used as a guide to values only. Regional pricing differences exist. In many cases we have noted the state where a piece was found. Some articles sell better in one area of the country than in another. This influences prices since supply and demand is a basic factor in retailing. In general we have found residents in the West and Midwest to be more oak-oriented than those in the East.

If you are a new buyer, a friend who has furnished a home with oak may be willing to assist you in your search for shops that deal in oak furniture. When you start buying, select a small piece such as an oak commode. In the early 20th century this was the piece on which the family kept a washbowl and pitcher readily available so hands and faces could be washed at mealtimes. Currently such a piece enhances areas such as hallways, parlors, bedrooms or kitchens.

Bargain hunters should be cautious if a piece of oak furniture has been painted. Paint may be hiding damage to the top of a table or dresser. Following paint removal, a great deal of sanding may be needed to eliminate water rings or other damage disguised by the paint. Inspect prospective purchases well and take into account any repair work that a piece may require.

In your endeavor to learn about oak furniture **study** is the key word. Find books that deal with oak in your local library and bookstores. Visit antique shops in your area to inspect the various oak pieces and accessories that are on display and learn what is available. Old catalogs provide an excellent means to study the many varieties of pressed back chair designs available in the late 19th and early 20th centuries. Learn all you can about this attractive wood with the golden glow – a popular purchase in the late 1800s and still in style over one hundred years later.

Two sides of oak furniture—fancy and plain.
On the left is an elaborately carved golden oak sideboard with a grotesque design at the top. On the right, a simple Mission-style buffet. Both styles were popular at the turn of the century.

Chapter 1

The Hardy Oak and Its Look-Alikes

Sturdy, staunch, heavy, hard, hearty – that is oak. Literature has contributed to the belief that oak is strong since the mighty tree from a tiny acorn grows. Henry Wadsworth Longfellow, in his poem "The Village Blacksmith," depicts oak's cousin, the chestnut, as a gracious majestic giant. "Under the spreading chestnut tree the village smithy stands…" The gentle guardian shades visitors while a burly blacksmith sweats over his flame and anvil, pounding out glowing iron to shape wagon parts, farm tools, kitchen utensils, fireplace accessories, or horse shoes. Appropriately, it was actually a horse chestnut tree that inspired Longfellow.

In addition to chestnut, other trees including ash, elm, and hickory, resemble oak yet have distinguishing characteristics of their own. Occasionally, devotees might be surprised and perhaps not too pleased, to realize that some of their oak furniture is not oak at all. Because oak does not bend easily, curved parts such as the rounded back frames on chairs, are frequently formed of elm or hickory. Since oak tends to splinter when held to a lathe, turnings are usually made of a different wood. Many oak iceboxes are actually ash or elm. Because of the similarity in grain pattern, it is easy to let these look-alikes pass for oak when dealers and collectors label them incorrectly.

Wood Identification Terms

A discussion of terms used in this book will promote a greater understanding of woods.

Annual rings are a tree's concentric yearly growth rings. They go round and round inside the tree trunk in bull's eye fashion.

Grain is the arrangement and direction of fibers in wood that give the wood its markings or texture

Medullary or *pith rays* radiate from the center of the tree, almost in the way a kindergartner draws a yellow sun with straight yellow lines to represent rays. Oak's pith rays are referred to as flakes.

Pores are small openings for the absorption and discharge of fluids. When clearly visible, the wood is referred to as open-grain. Closed grain indicates pores that are difficult to see.

Plain-sawed refers to boards sliced from the whole log length-wise in parallel cuts. Stripes and a series of elliptical Vs are the resulting pattern.

Quarter-sawed is a term that comes from the early practice of cutting a log into quarters by splitting it in half length-wise. Each half was then cut in half again. The four equal triangles were sliced into parallel boards almost at right angles to the annual growth rings. This method wastes wood and calls for extra processing which increases the cost but produces lumber, which shrinks and warps less than plain-sawed wood. Also, quarter-sawing vividly exposes the flakes or pith rays to produce a pronounced pattern.

Characteristics of Indigenous Furniture Woods

Ash, an open-grained wood, has a prominent grain that resembles oak. It is heavy, dense, and light-colored. Because of its great strength, ash was formerly used for wagon wheels that rolled pioneers across America's plains. Many "oak" iceboxes are actually made of ash. Upholstery frames are also often made from this strong wood.

Chestnut is grayish brown in appearance and has a coarse, open grain. It is softer, lacks large rays, and is not as structurally strong as oak. A fungus disease attacked and destroyed most of the nation's chestnut trees, but companies turned the carnage into profit by dubbing the lumber "wormy chestnut" and making attractive panels from it.

Elm, a close-grained wood, bends with ease and lends itself well to furniture parts that are curved. It is porous with an oak-like texture. Because the wood has pleasing figures, and its tendency to warp needs to be controlled, it is a natural choice for veneers. It does not split readily, so turned parts can be fashioned from elm. Chair seats were frequently constructed from this wood.

Hickory is hard and refuses to work easily, but shares the color and texture of oak. It is strong, elastic, and good for bent parts, especially those requiring both thinness and strength such as bow-backs on chairs. In former years, it was used to make staunch wagon wheel spokes. Today, tool handles are made of hickory.

Oak is light in color but heavy, hard, durable, coarse and open-grained. Its large pores are readily seen. Distinct pith rays, called flakes, show up in the quarter-sawed lumber and are one of the largest rays in any tree native to the United States. Oak was the favorite furniture wood in the late 1800s and the early 1900s. When plain-sawed, elliptical Vs are often seen in the resulting pattern. Shivering oak trees refuse to grow in extremely cold climates. Nevertheless, approximately 275 oak varieties are rooted in many countries. There are 60 types in the United States; with only about 14 used for the construction of commercial furnishings. While oaks grow throughout the entire country, most oak furniture comes from east of the Great Plains.

Artificial grain is not a wood itself, but refers to inexpensive woods with little or no pattern that have been stained to emulate oak. Small-town hotels, which required a commode in every room, could buy such furniture more economically than they could oak. Families who wanted to be up-to-date, but could not afford genuine oak, could choose this imitation.

The 1897 Sears, Roebuck and Company catalog, the style pacesetter for the masses, boldly presented elm or ash in an "antique oak" finish. Often times, the base wood was not specified but described as constructed of "the best selected material," finished in "antique oak."

How do you dress elm or ash or other hardwoods in antique oak guise? David W. Kendall, one of Grand Rapids, Michigan's first furniture designers, discovered the answer in the late 1800s. He observed that workers chewed tobacco, spitting the messy juice on the oak floor of the factories. This expulsion darkened the boards. Kendall tried rubbing a tobacco liquid on furniture, but the resulting stain was not permanent. Chemicals were used to obtain the desired appearance. Jealous competitors christened this finish "mud," but they hastened to achieve a similar color when antique oak became a marketable commodity.

The 1908 Sears catalog offered a new cupboard design in "hardwood with solid oak front, high gloss golden finish." Most of the iceboxes illustrated were made of elm and were given a similar finish. Hotel commode washstands, made of northern hardwoods, also wore golden oak makeup.

By 1927, thirty years after the first Sears description of "antique oak" furniture, dining room sets "soundly constructed of hardwood, in imitation of quarter-sawed oak" were "good looking and thoroughly reliable." Golden or fumed finishes were prominent.

In order to detect faked graining, look at the inside of a solid wood drawer-front and note whether the pattern has similar characteristics on both sides. On a stand or table, check underneath the top for this same feature.

Golden Oak. This moniker must have been inspired by a salesman who wanted to create allure and aura for a wood which he hoped to promote as walnut's stand-in. Why? By 1880, the supply of walnut in the United States was almost depleted, and a replacement was needed. Popularity is peculiar and fickle. Oak was adopted as the pet wood or those seeking to be modern. Rich ornamentation with applied carving bid adieu, as simpler, less cluttered furniture gracefully entered the marketplace.

If you desire to add to your knowledge of oak furniture, visit Grand Rapids, Michigan. Grand Rapids was the furniture capital of the United States during the last half of the nineteenth century. Tiptoe into the research section of the downtown public library and talk with the knowledgeable staff. Original catalogs, kept on file, are a trifle crisp and fragile, but when handled gently will reveal a glimpse of yesteryear. Walnut eagerly dominates, but oak, a late 1800s newcomer, shows its presence.

In 1890, the Manestee Manufacturing Company of Grand Rapids advertised an oversized golden oak sideboard with a top four feet long and almost three feet deep at a price of $14.00. It was finished in layers of shellac with a coloring agent added. After each layer dried, other layers were added, then rubbed to emit a golden glow. In 1893, the Widdicomb Furniture Company in Grand Rapids offered bedroom and dining room suites in oak, bird's-eye maple, and curly birch. By 1895, Widdicomb's descriptive terminology switched to white oak, golden oak or birch, and mahogany, as people of the Gay Nineties updated their home furnishings, tossed out the clutter of the immediate past, and lightened their dark, heavily draped rooms to let in the golden sunshine.

Chapter 2

The Entry Hall

Earlier generations referred to the hall at the entrance of a modern home as a vestibule. This hallway acts as a home's silent greeter, welcoming people and inviting them in. Do you want your home to be unique? Do you want your décor to exude warmth and friendliness so visitors feel welcome? An attractive and welcoming entrance with a difference can be achieved when antiques are featured.

Before closets were prevalent in the entrance hall, the hall tree or hall rack was an important utilitarian item. A common version consisted of a tall, standing frame with a series of hooks for hanging outer garments such as hats, coats, scarves, and stoles.

More elaborate hall trees provided a mirror for adjusting hair and hats, and a bench on which to sit while removing or donning overshoes. If this seat had a hinged lid over a storage box, the hall tree had an additional function. Depending on the family's needs, this area was a hideout for articles such as boots, scarves, and mittens. Some versions even included drawers.

Usefulness of the hall rack was further increased when arms circled out to hold erect rain-drenched umbrellas. Removable metal pans, frequently with cast designs or ornamental shapes, were placed at the base to catch any drips.

If the hall rack was top heavy, it was attached to the wall to keep it from falling forward. An examination of photographs in this chapter shows hall trees with different features, including moldings, shaped strips of wood used for ornamental purposes, applied decorations, hand crafted carvings, and crowned pediments. If a large rack proves to be overpowering in a small entryway, a mirror with hooks in its surrounding frame could serve as a coat and hat receiver.

The giant hall tree pictured on page 14 would demand a large area in a hallway to show off its appendages. A beveled mirror provides adequate viewing space and its frame is graced with embossed leaves and scrolls. Two massive, carved, imaginary animals form the arms of the boxed base. The figures have the head, mane, and feet of an animal, plus exotic wings and a dragon-type tail. This mythological creature is called a chimera or chimaera, evolving from a fire-breathing monster that possessed a lion's head, a scaly toad's body, and a tail.

Creative modern housewives no longer restrict these pieces to hall duty. The furnishings with hooks serve in the bathroom as towel holders, or as a place to hang garments while one showers. A lift lid becomes a hideaway for toilet supplies.

A separate hall bench frequently stood with its back to the wall, and its hinged seat doubled as a storage compartment. A set resulted when a framed mirror of like wood and a comparable design hung on the wall above the bench. Notice the center back panel of the bench with the grotesque on page 18. The seat's short legs terminate in paw feet. A molding tops this example, and applied carving shows well on the arms. One illustrated bench has various decorative features, including beading, both applied and incised carving, and paw feet – a feature that resembles animals' paws. Beading, used for decorative purposes, is another example of molding. It resembles a series of beads in a row.

Hall benches, when moved out of their intended habitats, can provide additional seating anywhere in the house. Country-oriented pillow animals or fowl, fashioned from salvaged pieces of worn quilts or coverlets, may adorn their surfaces. These worn covers are called *cutters* by the trade and are sold for such projects.

Many of these benches were paired with a framed mirror of similar design. Hooks were secured in the mirror frame, providing additional space for hanging hats.

Hall tree with lift-lid bench, 4 double hat hooks and applied decorations; 30" arm to arm, 16" deep, 80" high. $1,395.

Hall tree with lift-lid bench, 4 double hat hooks and applied decorations; 25" wide, 16" deep, 80" high. $845.

Hall tree with lift-lid bench, 4 double hat hooks and applied decorations; 31" arm to arm, 16" deep, 82" high. $795.

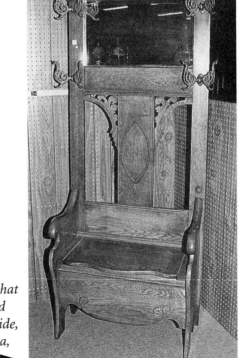

Hall tree with lift-lid, four hat and coat hooks, mirror and applied decorations; 29" wide, 16" deep, 78" high. In Iowa, $1,250.

Hall tree with two hat and coat hooks and applied decorations; 28" wide, 18" deep, 77" high. In Michigan, $795.

Hall tree with lift-lid storage compartment (sometimes listed in early catalogues as a "lid to set for rubbers" or "to hold rubbers, etc.") 29" arm to arm, 16" deep, 78 1/2" high. In Iowa, $995.

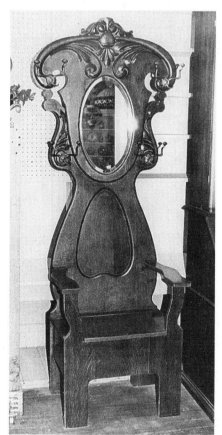

Hall tree with lift-lid storage compartment, brass hat hooks, inverted heart design, and applied decorations; 25 1/2" arm to arm, 17 1/2" deep, 77" high. In Illinois, $995.

Hall tree with lift-lid storage compartment, brass hat hooks, applied decorations, and shell design at crest; 33" wide, 17" deep, 84" high. In Illinois, $945.

Hall tree with lift-lid storage compartment, ornate leaf carving, brass hat hooks, and carved imaginary animals called chimeras (wild beasts of the imagination) that form the arms; 54 1/2" wide, 20 1/2" deep, 89" high. In Illinois, $3,750.

Close-up of chimera on hall tree.

Church or lodge chair with upholstered seat and back panel; 31" arm to arm, 26" deep, 72" high. In Indiana, $395.

Hall tree with lift-lid storage compartment; 36" arm to arm, 15 1/2" deep, 81" high. In Wisconsin, $1,250.

Hall tree with lift-lid bench, four hat and coat hooks and applied decorations; 38" arm to arm, 16" deep, 81" high. In Illinois, $1,295.

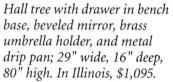

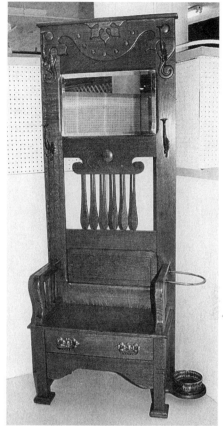

Hall tree with drawer in bench base, beveled mirror, brass umbrella holder, and metal drip pan; 29" wide, 16" deep, 80" high. In Illinois, $1,095.

Hall tree with lift-lid bench, four hat and coat hooks and beveled mirror; 44" wide, 18" deep, 85" high. In Michigan, $1,795.

Hall tree with lift-lid storage compartment, brass drip pan, and applied decorations; 35" arm to arm, 17" deep, 78 1/2" high. In Iowa, $1,950.

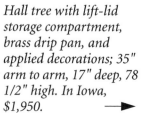

ENTRY

Hall tree with lift-lid storage compartment, metal umbrella holder, and beveled mirror; 28" wide, 14" deep, 75" high. In Illinois, $945.

Hall tree with lift-lid bench, four hat and coat hooks and applied decorations; 30" arm to arm, 16" deep, 77" high. In Illinois, $875.

Pier mirror with applied decorations and carvings; 26" wide, 88" high with 8" shelf depth. $1,250.

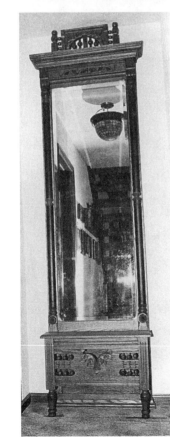

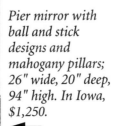

Pier mirror with ball and stick designs and mahogany pillars; 26" wide, 20" deep, 94" high. In Iowa, $1,250.

Hall tree with lift-lid storage compartment, beveled mirror, and applied decorations near and on pediment top: 27" wide, 16" deep, 78" high. In Ohio, $945.

Cherry and oak lift-lid hall bench with applied decorations; 36" wide, 20" deep, 39" high. $495.

Lift-lid hall bench and accompanying beveled mirror with 4 double hooks; bench, 39" wide, 17" deep, 38" high; mirror, 36" wide, 24" high. $925.

Lift-lid hall bench and accompanying mirror with 4 double hooks and applied decorations; Bench is 52" wide, 19" deep, 38" high. Mirror is 53" wide, 27" deep. $2,595. →

Hall bench with applied decorations and lift-lid storage compartment. Originally the base section of a large hall tree; 40" wide, 18" deep, 32" high. In Illinois, $475.

Hall bench with lift-lid storage compartment, paw feet, and grotesque open-mouth heads on arms and back panel; 46" wide, 18" deep, 43" high. In Iowa, $895.

Two-piece hall tree with lift-lid bench and paw feet (left); 41" wide, 17" deep, 39" high. Accompanying oval mirror (right) with four hat and coat hooks; 37" wide, 25" high. In Michigan, $1,395 for the two-piece set.

Hall mirror with four hat hooks; 20" wide, 34" high. In Illinois, $245.

Mirror with 2 double hat hooks, beveled mirror, and applied decorations; 36" wide, 72" high. $395.

Hall mirror with 4 double hat hooks, beveled mirror, and applied decorations; 23" wide, 32" high. $245.

Hall mirror with 4 double hat hooks; 23" wide, 33" high. $265.

Hall mirror with hat hooks, beading, and applied decoration; 33" x 33". In Iowa, $250.

Hall mirror with three double hat hooks and applied beading; 18" square. $315.

Hall mirror with 4 copper-washed hat hooks; 30" wide, 21" high. $255.

Hall mirror with 4 double hat hooks; 34" wide, 22" high. $265.

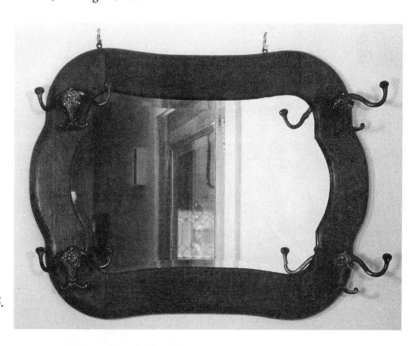

Hall mirror with 4 double hat hooks; 33" wide, 22" high. $285.
→

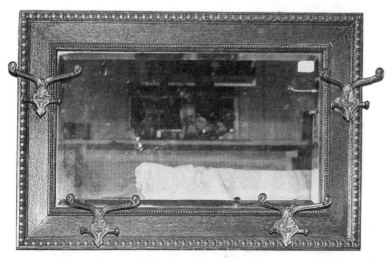

Hall mirror with 4 double hat hooks and applied edge beading; 30" wide, 20" high. $265.
←

Double hall mirror with iron hat hooks; 26" x 15 1/4". In Iowa, $395.

Hall mirror with iron hat hooks; 29" x 19". In Wisconsin, $245. ⟵

Hall mirror with 4 copper-washed hat hooks; 30" wide, 21" high. $255. ⟶

School coat and hat rack with a label that reads "Odell's Hat and Coat Rack, pat. Nov. 1, '87 mfg. by the Odell Iron Works, Indianapolis"; 24" wide, 7" deep. $195.

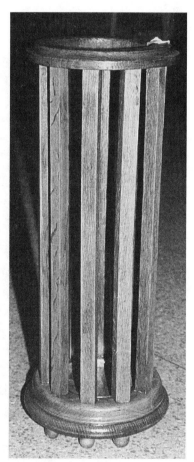

Hat and umbrella rack with tin drip pan and 2 replaced brass hat hooks; 15" wide, 14" deep, 68" high. $345.

Umbrella stand converted into a hanging light; 8 1/2" square, 25" high. In Wisconsin, $225.

Umbrella stand with a mission influence; 10" diameter, 25 1/2" high. In Iowa, $185.

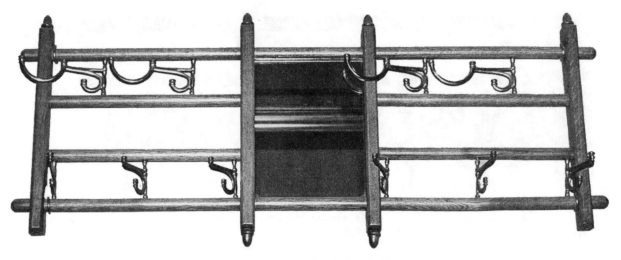

Hat rack with mirror and ten brass swivel hooks; 35 1/2" x 15". In Iowa, $225.

Umbrella stand; 12" square, 27" high. In Ohio, $145.

Umbrella stand; 13" square, 30" high. In Illinois, $165.

Chapter 3

The Living Room

The parlor, as the living room was called in the 1800s, was a room where special guests, such as the parson or priest, visiting friends, the daughter's beau, or business acquaintances, were entertained. The parlor was reserved for visits by these special people and was not a place where the family gathered, as in the living room of today. Editorials in women's magazines at the turn of the century began to deplore this tradition, and argued that the residents of the home were more important than guests who came and went. As a consequence, the family oriented living room was born. Commonly associated with this room were particular pieces of furniture.

Rocking chairs, one of the components of this room, were popular with Americans, who liked the gentle, swaying motion of the chair. Europeans, however, felt insecure in these rockers, fearing they would tip over and injure themselves. Housewives were often distressed with the rocking motion that tended to wear out rugs. To counteract these problems, various patented chairs, called "patent" or "platform" rockers, which swayed on attached foundations or platforms, were developed. Occasionally, a patent date can be found on the metal parts in the base of the rocker. Other types of rockers were built with or without arms; with upholstered, cane, wooden, or rush seats; with pressed, splat, slat, and spindled backs. Rocking chairs serving special functions were also developed, such as sewing or slipper rockers.

Upholstered furniture was available for living room comfort, and included fainting couches with a built-in pillow at one end. Another variety of couch, known as a bed lounge, had arms that folded down to provide a sleeping space. Some couches featured a pullout section that doubled the reclining area. Another type provided a storage site for bedding. Sofas that could be converted into beds were popular with homemakers. Parlor suites, having as many as ten pieces, could include a divan, armchair, parlor chair, rocker, sofa and a few side chairs.

Before coil springs were invented in France during the reign of Louis XV (1715-1774), feathers, animal hair, or other stuffing materials, supported by webbing, softened the backs and seats of chairs. Metal springs, when added, were cushioned with hair and cotton batting. Golden oak furniture used plush, velour, brocaded silk, damask, and both real and imitation leather as upholstery materials.

Lamp tables were abundant because many homes were not electrified in the early part of the 1900s. These tables provided a place for kerosene lamps or in some instances, a candle. Another kind of table was called the parlor table, which had oval, square, rectangular, and cloverleaf tops, and many had base shelves. Leg shapes varied from cabriole, reeded, fluted, to straight types, some of which terminated in paw or claw feet. Applied decorations and carving, real carving, and incised lines and designs gave each table an individual character.

Today, electric lights are accepted as a necessary item in such places as homes, business locations, restaurants, hospitals, and hotels. Before electricity was prevalent, however, kerosene lamps sat on tables or hung from ceilings and provided a wavering light. Candles, too, had their place on various stands and tables throughout the home, and lights that did not hang needed a table or stand to sit upon.

On October 19, 1879, Thomas Edison's incandescent bulb began to glow. Later, city dwellers whose streets were lit by Edison's invention were delighted and excited. It was considered remarkable when, in 1892, those who attended the Columbia Exposition in Chicago thought Edison's lights recreated daylight. At the 1892 Colombian Exhibition in Chicago, many parlor tables held electric lamps. Their styles varied. Some featured graceful French legs while others showed splayed legs (slanted out) with glass balls held by claw feet. During this time-span, parlor tables were available in many styles, most of which are pictured in this book. City homes soon had electricity, and, in the 1930s, the United States government began rural electrification projects. This development greatly increased the use of parlor tables.

During this transition period, individual lamps were made with a dual purpose. They could either burn kerosene or be converted to electric power with the necessary attachments. Parlor tables with round, rectangular, or square tops proved to be a popular site for lamps. Plant stands and lamp stands held not only kerosene lamps but candles as well. Stands comparable in size held floral displays. These were called plant stands or pedestals.

Grand Rapids, Michigan was America's furniture capital in the late 1800s. Research by the authors at the Grand Rapids Public Library revealed that more than 85 furniture manufacturers started in business there. One of these was the Stickley Brothers Company. The brothers, working together, created furniture characteristic of that period. Brothers Leopold and J. George Stickley opened furniture-manufacturing plants in New York state. Albert became the president of Stickley Brothers Company.

A Quaint Furniture metal tag, shown in this chapter, identifies a folding parlor table marked Stickley Bros. Co., Grand Rapids, Mich. Other Stickley furniture can be found in this book under the headings, "The Arts and Crafts Movement" and "Mission Furniture."

Platform rocker with applied beading and decorations; 23" arm to arm, 38" high, $395.

Platform rocker with pressed top rail and slats; 23" arm to arm, 42" high, $425.

Platform or patent rocker with upholstered seat and back; 29" arm to arm, 36" high. In Pennsylvania, $545.

Platform rocker with upholstered seat and back; 22" arm to arm, 38" high. In Iowa, $285.

Platform rocker with upholstered seat and back; 25" arm to arm, 37" high. In Wisconsin, $425.

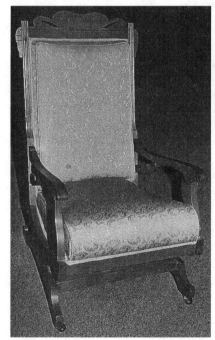

Two-piece parlor set consisting of platform rocker - 23" arm to arm, 39" high; and loveseat . In Iowa, $545 for the two-piece set. (Loveseat on p. 32)

Platform rocker with upholstered back, seat and arm rests; 26" arm to arm, 36" high. In Illinois, $425.

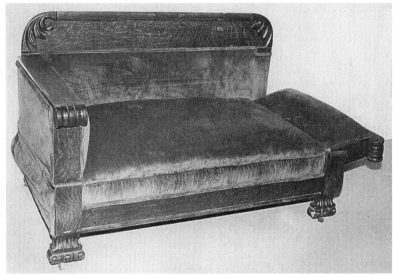

Couch, circa 1889, with arms that fold down; 55" arm to arm, 31" deep, 34" high, $595.

Couch, often called a fainting couch or chaise lounge, with stepback and applied decorations; 72" long, 21" deep, 34" high. In Illinois, $695.

Couch with upholstered seat, sides, and backs, and side arms that lower for conversion into a bed; 59" wide, 28" deep, 39" high, $465.

Three-piece parlor set consisting of rocker - 27" arm to arm, 36" high; settee or sofa - 49" arm to arm, 37" high; and arm chair - 27" arm to arm, 36" high. In Iowa, $895 for the three-piece set.

Cane-seat settee; 47" arm to arm, 18" deep, 38" high. In Kentucky, $595.

Settee with incised carving; 46" arm to arm, 22" deep, 40" high, $695.

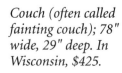

Couch (often called fainting couch); 78" wide, 29" deep. In Wisconsin, $425.

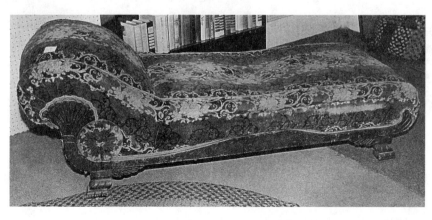

LIVING ROOM

Sofa; 47" wide, 39" high. In Iowa, $625.

Love seat with upholstered seat and back panels and applied decorations on rail and splat; 36" arm to arm, 23" deep, 40" high. In Wisconsin, $425.

Side chair with upholstered seat and back panel; 43" high. In Tennessee, $1,195.

Sofa that converts into a double bed with black tufted leatherlike upholstery, scrolled arms and legs, serpentine base and claw feet; 83" arm to arm, 36" deep, 44" high, $3,250.

LIVING ROOM

Grotesque between the front legs of an upholstered armchair.

Love seat; 44" arm to arm, 20" deep, 41" high. In Iowa, $425.

Side chair with upholstered seat and back and applied decorations, 41" high. In Michigan, $255.

Divan with armrest and pierced carving in back; 26" wide, 33" high. In Colorado, $425.

Carved-back love seat with upholstered seat and back; 34" arm to arm, 38" high. In Illinois, $495.

Female finial on the left backpost of an upholstered chair.

Male finial on the right back post of an upholstered chair.

Loveseat from two-piece parlor set, 52" arm to arm, 36" high. In Iowa, $545 for the two-piece set. (Platform rocker on p. 27)

Love seat with upholstered seat and back; 38" arm to arm, 22" deep, 36" high. In Iowa, $445.

Parlor table with scalloped top, base shelf, and turned legs; 30" wide, 22" deep, 29" high, $265.

Plain-sawed oak parlor table showing elliptical Vs; 23" by 24", 30" high, $195.

Parlor table with cut-out provision in top and lower shelf for chair; 26" wide, 20" deep, 29" high, $365.

Parlor table with octagonal top, scalloped base shelf, and twisted legs; 26" wide, 29" high, $385.

Parlor table with beading on base shelf and apron, twisted legs, and one-piece brass ball and claw feet; 30" square, 30" high, $595.

Parlor table with applied decorations, incised designs, and reeded legs; 28" square, 30" high, $455.

Parlor table with scalloped top, twist-turned legs, and shelf that is attached to the legs with metal brackets; 23" square, 29" high, $245.

Parlor table with serpentine apron, scalloped top, and base shelf; 24" square, 30" high, $495.

*Parlor table with ball-and-stick apron design; 22"
square, 30" high. In Michigan, $295.*

*Parlor table with beading and ball and claw feet; 24"
square, 30" high. $275.*

*Parlor table with pedestal base; 24" square, 30" high.
In Michigan, $345.*

*Parlor table with claw and glass-ball feet; 29" diameter,
29" high. In Iowa, $650.*

Parlor table with ball-and-stick-design apron under top; 23" square, 29" high. In Wisconsin, $345.

Parlor table with scalloped edges; 24" square, 27 1/2" high. In Illinois, $375.

Parlor table with cabriole legs and base shelf; 24" diameter, 30" high. In Michigan, $265.

LIVING ROOM

Folding table; 24" square, 27 1/2" high. In Illinois, $215.

Tilt-top table, which is rarely found in oak; 22" wide, 18" deep, 28" high. In Illinois, $445.

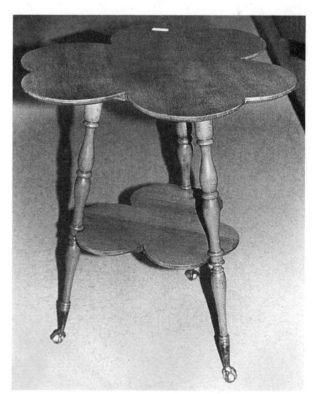

Parlor table with cloverleaf top and lower shelf; 27" square, 29 1/2" high. In Virginia, $295.

Oval parlor table with carving at top of cabriole legs; 40" wide, 26" deep, 30" high. In Virginia, $395.

←

Plant stand with scroll feet; 12" diameter, 18" high. In Wisconsin, $245.

Parlor table with cloverleaf top, round base shelf and beading on legs; 17" wide, 29" high. In Michigan, $275.

Close-up of child's head on apron of parlor table.

Parlor table with ornately carved legs, applied decoration, and carved child's head on apron; 29" wide, 16" deep, 29 1/2" high. In Illinois, $750.

Parlor table with carved relief heads on drawer and apron ends; 26" x 19", 29" high. In Illinois, $675.

Plant stand with cabriole legs; 12" square, 18" high. In Iowa, $235.

LIVING ROOM

Tilt-top pedestal table from the 1920s with brass caps on feet; 40: diameter, 29" high. In Kentucky, $455.

←

A cut-down round oak table that has been made into a lazy Susan with a top that rotates; 42" diameter, 18" high, $495.

Radio table that provides space for speakers on base shelf; 27" wide, 19" deep, 29" high. In Michigan, $345.

Parlor table with glass ball and claw feet; 27" square, 29 1/2" high. In Illinois, $495.

Palette table made to resemble artist's palette; 28" wide, 24" deep, 29" high. In Michigan, $450.

Parlor table with cabriole legs and applied designs on apron; 30" wide, 22" deep, 29" high. In Michigan, $425.

Quarter-sawed oak parlor table with double top, round column legs and base shelf; 24" square, 29" high. In Michigan, $350.

Parlor table with octagonal scalloped top and reeded legs; 20" wide, 20" deep, 30" high. In Michigan, $325.

Victorian oval parlor table with ash top and walnut base accented with center-support column, spindles, and applied decorations made of ash; 14" wide, 26" deep, 31" high. In Wisconsin, $455.

Quarter-sawed oak parlor table with glass balls held by metal claw feet; 22" square, 29" high. In Tennessee, $425.

Octagonal parlor table with twisted legs; 27" wide, 29" high. In Illinois, $355.

Quarter-sawed oak pedestal table with Empire scroll feet; 24" diameter, 29" high. In Wisconsin, $275.

Parlor table with two pillars and scroll feet; 38" wide, 25" deep, 29" high. In Michigan, $525.

Lamp table with splayed legs and shelf at base; 18" square, 31" high. In Michigan, $245.

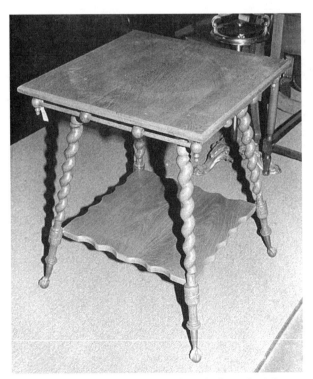

Parlor table with splayed rope legs, ball-and-stick apron and scalloped-bottom shelf; 24" square, 30" high. In Indiana, $345.

Taboret or plant stand with scalloped top; 12" square, 15" high, $195.

Plant stand with splayed legs and base shelf; 16" square, 31" high, $195.

Taboret or plant stand with hexagonal top and ball and stick design between legs; 14" square, 21" high, $195.

Plant stand with hexagonal top; 14" square, 20" high, $195.

Plant stand with oak top and French leg iron base; 14" diameter, 28 1/4" high. In Iowa, $355.

Lamp or plant stand with splayed legs; 16" diameter, 29" high. In Illinois, $225.

Plant or lamp stand with splayed legs; 18" square, 28" high. In Iowa, $245.

Taboret or short plant stand; 15" diameter, 20" high. In Illinois, $135.

LIVING ROOM

Octagonal pedestal or plant stand; 12" wide, 37" high. In Iowa, $245.

Pedestal plant stand; 14" diameter, 36" high. In Wisconsin, $235.

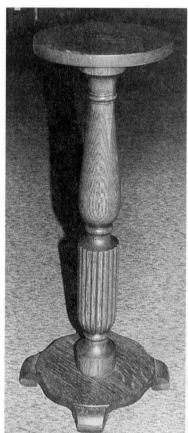

Pedestal plant stand; 12" diameter, 34" high. In Iowa, $245.

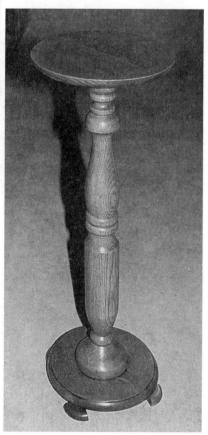

Pedestal stand; 12" diameter, 30" high. In Wisconsin, $245.

Plant stand; 13" diameter, 34" high. In Illinois, $225.

Plant stand; 13" square top; 33" high. In Michigan, $245. ←

Taboret or plant stand with keyhole design in legs; 12" square, 19" high, $195. →

Fern stand with applied gesso decorations in panels; 18" x 13", 37" high. In Indiana, $360. ←

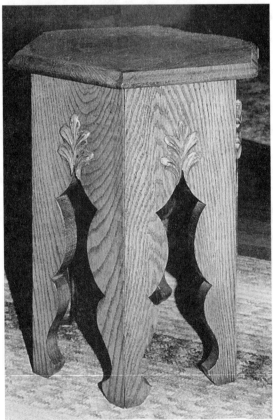

Taboret (or plant stand); 12" wide, 18" high. In Iowa, $185.

Parlor table or lamp stand; 16" square, 32" high. In Wisconsin, $295.

Plant stand with oval top; 16" wide, 11" deep, 30" high. In Michigan, $195. →

Plant stand; 12" square top, 36" high. In Michigan, $225.

Pedestal plant stand; 13" diameter, 34 1/2" high. In Wisconsin, $265.

Pedestal plant stand; 12" diameter, 29 1/2" high. In Illinois, $265.

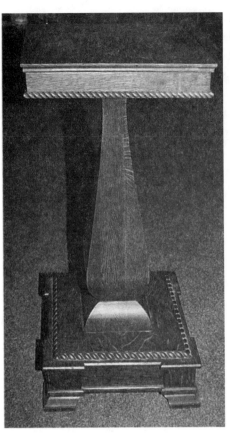

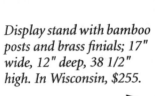

Fern stand; 17" square, 39" high. In Indiana, $425.

Display stand with bamboo posts and brass finials; 17" wide, 12" deep, 38 1/2" high. In Wisconsin, $255.

Plant stand; 12" wide, 16 1/4" high. In Iowa, $185.

Lamp or plant stand with brass feet; 17" square, 30" high. In Wisconsin, $625.

Chapter 4

The Dining Room

In the late summer and early fall, farmers joined forces to harvest their crops – going to a different farm each weekday. The men and boys worked outside, while the women and girls prepared a sumptuous meal. Large, sturdy round or square tables were extended, and, with leaves inserted, were spacious enough for the workers to sit around laughing and telling stories as they ate.

Tables designed to seat large families could be either square with heavy legs or round with pedestal bases. Literature from the Grand Rapids, Michigan library states that Stowe and Davis marketed a pillar extension table in 1887. Early varieties were constructed from plain-sawed oak. However, when demand increased, they were offered in quarter-sawed oak, walnut, and mahogany. They wholesaled at a low fifty to seventy-five cents a running foot, and were available in various sizes from six to twelve feet, when extended.

The 1897 Sears catalog featured a round, drop-leaf table with five legs. The six-foot size cost $3.40. The larger ten-foot table sold for $5.00. Six other tables pictured were square. Those made of ash were the least expensive. However, one $5.28 ash example extended to twelve feet. The most expensive oak table in this size was listed at $17.50. Fancy brackets connected the two legs at each end, and the middle leg helped support additional leaves.

When wares were shipped in freight trains from Sears or other catalog centers, there was an additional cost. Many were sent "knocked down", and the buyer received specific instructions on how to assemble their new table.

Furniture names sometimes change over time. Yesterday's round pillar tables are today referred to as pedestal tables. In 1902, Sears advertised old-fashioned round, drop-leaf extension tables as well as oak round pillar tables. A plain twelve-foot expanding table cost $11.50. More expensive versions, made of quarter-sawed oak, featured beaded molding on the apron. Carved and ornamental legs extended from the center pillar and ended in paw feet.

Square top oak extension tables with five legs were also available. Currently, round extension tables sell more readily than the square versions.

Sideboards or buffets provide storage areas for items such as china, glass, linens and silverware. The terms are more or less interchangeable; in this book, "sideboard" describes the more elaborate units, and "buffet" is used for the simpler versions. Today, china buffet is the name assigned to a combination buffet and china cabinet. A china buffet includes both doors and drawers, as well as glassed-in sides or fronts that display the china and crystal.

A most unusual china cabinet is pictured in this chapter on page 82. Serpentine glass (S-curved) panels are found on the sides as well as in the door. Two columns, wooden carvings of women, support the top shelf. This is an adaptation of an early Greek architectural design where carved human figures formed supporting pillars. Female versions are called caryatids, while the male figures bear the name Atlantis. The feet of these cabinets displayed various styles, including paws, glass balls held by claws, and scroll versions. Most glass surfaces were advertised as "double thick," which increased their ability to survive unbroken. Perhaps the rarest cabinets are those designed for corner use. Many examples of this style are pictured in this chapter. A corner cupboard, naturally, was so named because it fit into a corner. When purchasing a corner cupboard, be sure it will fit into the space assigned to it.

China cabinets have glass panels allowing the owner to display prize china and glass. These cabinets may have flat, concave, or convex sides, but the latter is the most popular of the three. "Bent glass" was an early catalog term for these curved glass surfaces.

DINING ROOM

Various structural features that enhance the value of buffets, sideboards, and cabinets include the following:

>*Decorations* such as scrolls, beads, leaves, garlands, and medallions that are made separately and applied to the pieces.
>
>*Grotesques* are figures of animals or people intermixed with flowers, fruits, or foliage in an unnatural way. They can be applied to, or carved into, the pieces.
>
>When drawers project outward over the base, these cabinets are said to have *projection fronts*.
>
>*Serpentine drawers* curve in and out like a snake in motion.
>
>*Pilasters* are pillars sliced in half length-wise and applied to the furniture.
>
>*Scroll columns* and feet recall the heavy Empire style of the early 1800s.

Small serving carts are useful when drinks and desserts are served to the dinner guests. Also present in the dining room are large sideboards with ornate decorations and carvings. They hold china, silver, and glassware used at the dinner table.

Plate rails are shelves with ridges and a protective bar. They show off attractive china properly in kitchen or dining areas. What better place to expose grandma's treasured Deldare Ware, Tea Leaf, or Lenox china to public view than on a plate rail?

Extension table with lion's heads and paw-feet leg structure, and four 11" leaves; 52" x 59" with two leaves in position, 29" high. In Wisconsin, $3,150.

Square extension table with six bulbous reeded legs and concave stretchers with ball decorations; 44" square, 29" high, $995.
→

Round pedestal extension table; 54" diameter, 30" high, $995.
←

54" diameter table with the pedestal divided.
→

Square extension table with center support leg, paw feet, and six leaves; 44" square, 30" high, $1,050.

Double pedestal extension table with veneered apron and pedestal; 42" square, 30" high, $895.

Square extension table with center support leg; 42" square, 31" high, $485.

Queen Anne extension table with two center legs that remain stationary when the leaves are added, made by "Spencer Table and Chair Co., Marion, Ind."; 45" by 55", 30" high, $645.

Square extension table with five reeded legs; 42" square, 30" high, $495.

Extension table with center-leg support and two 10" leaves; 42" square, 30" high. In Iowa, $725.

Round pedestal extension table with beading on apron and paw feet; 45" diameter, 30" high, $1,150.

Round extension table with double pedestal base and paw feet; 45" diameter, 30" high, $1,550.

Round pedestal extension table with paw feet; 45" diameter, 29" high, $1,375.

Pedestal base for extension table with lion heads and paw feet. Complete table is $2,150.

Extension table with center supporting leg; 42" square, 28" high with four leaves, each 12" wide. In Wisconsin, $995.

Extension table with one 15" leaf, center support pillar and paw feet; 48" diameter, 30" high. In Michigan, $1,450.

Round pedestal extension table has two auxiliary supporting legs that drop down on each side when the table is opened, and scroll feet; 48" diameter, 29" high, $745.

Extension table with pedestal base, legs that pull out to extend table and three 11" leaves; 48" diameter, 30" high. In Michigan, $1,250.

Extension table with two center support legs; 46" square, 29 1/2" high; six 12"-wide leaves enable the table to extend to 177". In Wisconsin, $1,150.

Draw or refectory table; 30" x 42", 30" high, and 12" pullout leaves. In Wisconsin, $545.

Pedestal dining table; 42" diameter, 30 1/2" high. In Iowa, $725. Set of four mission chairs, $300.

Extension table with self-storing leaf at each end and center-support leg; 44" square, 30" high. In Wisconsin, $995.

Quarter-sawed oak top and maple-legged extension table with center leg support and five leaves; 45" square, 30" high. In Alaska, $950.

Extension table with center supporting leg; 42" square, 28 1/2" high, four leaves, each 12" wide. In Iowa, $725. Set of four cane bottom chairs, $695.

Cut-down dining table with claw feet; 45" diameter, 17" high. In Michigan, $675.

Extension table supported by base with four carved lions' heads; 48" x 56" x 31" high. In Iowa, $3,500.

Close-up of lion's head with paw feet that serve as supports for extension table.

Pedestal extension table; 45" diameter, 30" high. In Illinois, $545. ➝

Pedestal table with four leaves; 48" diameter, 31" high. In Illinois, $895. ⬅

Round extension pedestal table with claw feet; 45" diameter, 30" high. In Illinois, $995. ➝

Eastlake elm dining table with three leaves in place measures 75" wide, 42" deep, 29" high. In Wisconsin, $990.

Round extension table and four single-pressed back chairs; 38" high, table 45" diameter, 29" high. In Iowa, $625 for a set of 4 chairs; $525 for table.

Pedestal extension table with square, unadorned base; 54" diameter, 29 1/4" high. In Colorado, $625. Golden oak pressed-back chairs, 39 1/2" high, $165 each.

Round extension double-pedestal table with paw feet; 42" diameter, 29" high. In Iowa, $795.

DINING ROOM

Round extension pedestal table with paw and ball feet and three 11" leaves; 59" wide, 48" deep with one leaf in position, 31" high. In Wisconsin, $1,995. →

Three examples of pedestal bases for extension tables. In Iowa, $1,750 for middle example. ←

Pedestal extension table with beading on apron, claw feet and one leaf; 41" diameter, 30" high. In Illinois, $750. →

Extension table with center leg support: 48" square, 29" high. In Illinois, $515.

Extension table with center-support leg and six leaves made by the "Kiel Manufacturing Company. Manufacturers of Tables, Kiel, Wisconsin." They also made cabinets for Atwater-Kent radios. In Iowa, $895.

Extension table with center-support leg and three leaves; 44" square, 29" high. In Wisconsin, $1,295.

Oak dining room set from 1920s. Draw table; 38" by 54", 30" high with 15" draw ends. One of five side chairs; 39" high. Host chair; 24" arm to arm, 39" high. Buffet; 59" wide, 20" deep, 36" high with 2" rail. The host chair features a paper label reading, "Showers Brothers Company, Bloomington, Ind., America's largest furniture makers. Bedroom, dining room, kitchen furniture." In Illinois, $1,150 for the eight-piece set.

DINING ROOM

DINING ROOM

Table, 42" square, 28" high with three 9 1/2" leaves. In Illinois, $395. Cane seat chairs with pressed-back design; 38 1/2" high; $80 each. One-piece stepback cupboard; 43 1/2" wide, 22 1/4" deep, 79" high, $545.

←

Extension table with center leg support; 42" square, 30" high. In Iowa, $750.

←

Extension dining room table from the early 1900s with pedestal base, twisted Jacobean-type legs and six leaves; 55" square, 30" high. Six chairs that originally had caned center backs; 43" high. Seven-piece set is $1,950. Tea cart near windows; 33" wide, 18" deep, 27" high, $355.

←

Sideboard with applied decorations and pillars supporting top shelf; 48" wide, 23" deep, 76" high, $1,450. ←

Sideboard with applied decorations, serpentine drawers, and paw feet; 45" wide, 21" deep, 79" high, $995. →

Sideboard with applied decorations and pillars supporting top shelf; 41" wide, 20" deep, 79" high, $845. ←

Sideboard with applied decorations; 40" wide, 19" deep, 74" high, $795. →

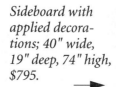

Sideboard with applied decorations and grotesque near the top; 48" wide, 24" deep, 77" high, $2,175. →

Sideboard with scroll shelf support and applied decorations; 48" wide, 22" deep, 64" high. In Illinois, $995. ←

Sideboard with applied decorations on bottom doors and serpentine-projection top drawers; 42" wide, 20" deep, 63" high, $1,150.

Sideboard with applied decorations and projection drawers; 44" wide, 22" deep, 77" high, $875. →

DINING ROOM

Sideboard with applied decorations on bottom doors; 46" wide, 23" deep, 65" high, $845.

China buffet with leaded glass and carved designs; 48" wide, 18" deep, 43" high. In Iowa, $875.

Buffet with scroll feet and candle brackets flanking mirror; 40" wide, 20" deep, 59" high, $655.

Sideboard with applied decorations, serpentine drawers, and shelves supported by scrolled pillars; 45" wide, 21" deep, 75" high, $875.

Buffet base from which veneer and artificial graining have been stripped except for the open door on the right that retains its quarter-sawed oak appearance; 46" wide, 21" deep, 36" high, $195.

Close up of a grotesque design found on a sideboard.

Worktable with carved designs on two doors; 41" wide, 20" deep, 32" high, $495.

Sideboard with applied decorations and grotesques on base doors and on top rail; 56" wide, 25" deep, 82" high. In Illinois, $2,150.

Marble-top sideboard with circa 1860 Victorian influence; 48" wide, 22" deep, 79 1/2" high. In South Carolina, $1,750.

Sideboard with serpentine drawers and applied decorations; 44" wide, 22" deep, 75" high. In Illinois, $1,450.

Sideboard with applied decoration on crest and doors; 42" wide, 20" deep, 72 1/2" high. In Connecticut, $995.

DINING ROOM

Oak sideboard in quarter-sawed oak; 48" wide, 20" deep, 52" high. In Illinois, $645.

Buffet or server with cabriole legs; 38" wide, 18" deep, 46" high, $565.

Buffet with applied decorations and open storage space near base; 45" wide, 21" deep, 58" high, $945.

Sideboard with swell-front top drawers, serpentine middle doors, and paw feet; 49" wide, 23" deep, 56" high. In Michigan, $595.

China buffet with serpentine drawers, two swell-projection drawers, and convex glass door: 46" wide, 20" deep, 40" high, $725.

China buffet with leaded glass and serpentine center drawer and doors; 54" wide, 20" deep, 40 1/2" high, 11 1/2" back rail. In Illinois, $1,450.

The carved lion's head and French paw foot are seen on a china buffet from the turn of the century, golden oak era; 27 1/4" high from head to foot.

China buffet with two convex glass china closets flanking central storage area; 62" wide, 21" deep, 70" high. In Illinois, $1,850.

China buffet with leaded glass in top door panel and convex glass doors; 49" wide, 20" deep, 64" high. In Michigan, $1,350.

Sideboard; 41" wide, 18" deep, 56" high. In South Carolina, $695.

China buffet with applied decoration; 42" wide, 19" deep, 58" high. In Iowa, $1,450.

Sideboard with serpentine projection front drawers; 42" wide, 21" deep, 79 1/4" high. In Georgia, $845.

Server with claw and ball front feet made by Grand Rapids Furniture Co.; 37" wide, 19" deep, 33" high with 4" rail. In Michigan, $615.

Sideboard with applied decoration; 52" wide, 23" deep, 76" high. In Maryland, $925.

Buffet with applied decorations, reeded pillars supporting top shelf, and serpentine top drawers; 42" wide, 21" deep, 76" high. In Iowa, $895.

Buffet with swell-projection top drawers, scroll feet and mirror supports, a style called "colonial" in the catalogs of the 1920s; 54" wide, 23" deep, 54" high, $645.

Sideboard with beveled mirror and applied decorations; 54" wide, 25" deep, 59" high. In Michigan, $795.

China buffet with serpentine doors and drawers; 53" wide, 22" deep, 71 1/2" high. In Illinois, $1,595.

China buffet with applied decoration on drawers and leaded glass on doors; 54" wide, 22" deep, 64" high. In Illinois, $1,750.

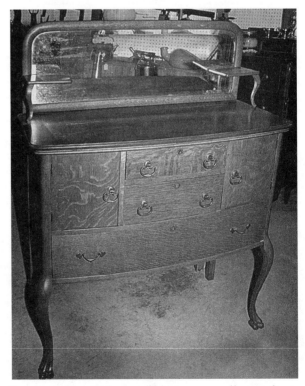

Server with swell front and lamp or candle stands at each side of rear mirror; 42" wide, 21" deep, 53" high. In Illinois, $595.

Server with swell top drawer and shelves for storage at each side; 48" wide, 18" deep, 41" high. In Iowa, $595.

Quarter-sawed oak server with bottom shelf; 42" wide, 21" deep, 42" high. In Tennessee, $495.

Sideboard with two swell drawers, applied and incised decorations, grotesque heads on shelf supports and beveled mirror; 50" wide, 22" deep, 66" high. In Illinois, $795.

Buffet with applied decorations and round columns with hoofed-type feet supporting the upper shelf; 48" wide, 22" deep, 76" high. In Iowa, $895.

China buffet with convex glass doors flanking the one-drawer and two-door center section; 54" wide, 19" deep, 59" high. In Michigan, $1,550.

China buffet with scrolled Empire feet and shelf supports and beveled mirror; 44" wide, 20" deep, 54" high; Seth Thomas mantel clock with artificial oak graining. In Wisconsin, buffet, $645, clock, $425.

China buffet with two glass china closets flanking an enclosed central storage area and a secret drawer at the base of the left side; 48" wide, 15" deep, 62" high. In Illinois, $1,395.

Buffet with applied decorations, swell top drawers and brass pulls, escutcheons and hinges; 50" wide, 24" deep, 74" high. In Indiana, $995.

DINING ROOM

DINING ROOM

China buffet with ogee top drawers and doors and serpentine base drawers, applied decorations, cabriole legs and paw feet; 53" wide, 22" deep, 69" high. In Illinois, $2,575.

Buffet with swell top drawers, beveled mirror and paw feet; 46" wide, 21" deep, 55" high. In Iowa, $595.

Server with swell drawer front, cabriole legs, paw feet and applied decoration on mirror top; 42" wide, 17" deep, 55" high. In Illinois, $565.

Buffet with applied decorations, grotesque upper-shelf support columns, three mirrors, and serpentine drawers; 48" wide, 23" deep, 85" high. In Indiana, $945.

China buffet with leaded glass doors, serpentine upper drawers, swell lower drawer, and beveled mirror; 45" wide, 21" deep, 56" high. In Wisconsin, $1,495.

Sideboard with swell-front center drawers, pressed designs on side doors and cabriole legs; 66" wide, 24" deep, 64" high. In Iowa, $1,495.

Quarter-sawed oak sideboard or buffet with grotesques on stiles and caryatid column supporting the top shelf; 54" wide, 24" deep, 67" high. In Indiana, $895.

Buffet with applied decorations, round upper-shelf support columns, serpentine drawers, and paw feet; 48" wide, 22" deep, 78" high. In Kentucky, $895.

L. and J.G. Stickley quarter-sawed oak sideboard with plate rail, pegged construction, and hand-hammered copper escutcheon plates and drawer pulls; 48" wide, 20" deep, 36" high, 8" plate rail, $1,350. →

Sideboard with swell top drawers, two paneled base drawers, applied decorations and paw feet; 60" wide, 25" deep, 67" high. In Kentucky, $1,250. →

Built-in buffet, photographed in a 1913 Arts and Crafts bungalow in Iowa, with flanking china cupboards and leaded glass doors; 139" wide, 57" high. →

DINING ROOM

DINING ROOM

China cabinet with hooded top, convex glass side panels, and paw feet, 39" wide, 14" deep, 75" high, $2,150.

China cabinet with convex glass in door and side panels and scroll feet, a style called "colonial" in the catalogs of the 1920s; 37" wide, 15" deep, 61" high, $1,145.

China cabinet with applied decorations and paw feet; 42" wide, 15" deep, 64" high, $1,150.

China cabinet with convex glass in door and side panels and paw feet; 42" wide, 14" deep, 66" high, $895.

China cabinet with convex glass in side panels and a straight glass door with muntins; 52" wide, 14" deep, 55" high, $895. →

China cabinet with convex glass in door and side panels; 40" wide, 14" deep, 63" high, $855. ←

China cabinet with convex glass side panels and paw feet; 40" wide, 14" deep, 60" high. In Michigan, $1,050.

China cabinet with convex door and side panels, applied grotesques above pillars; 34" wide, 12" deep, 62" high. In Virginia, $1,150.

Close-up of caryatid - the name applies to a female head used as a supporting column. If the head is male, it is called an atlantes. →

China cabinet with S-curved door and side glass, paw feet, and two intricately carved figures of women, called caryatids, holding up top shelf; 48" wide, 17" deep, 78" high. In Iowa, $6,500.

Corner china with two convex door panels; 37" wide, 21" deep, 66 1/2" high, 3 1/2" rail. In Wisconsin, $1,500.

DINING ROOM

China cabinet with two convex glass side panels, two convex glass door panels, and a front center door with designs on the glass; 46" wide, 17" deep, 77" high, $1,650. →

China cabinet with convex glass inside panels and in central door, pillars, leaded and beveled glass panels near top, applied decorations and paw feet; 47" wide, 17" deep, 76" high. In Texas, $2,650.

Corner china cabinet with concave door panel and applied decorations above glass panels; 36" wide, 23" deep, 72" high. In Indiana, $1,695. →

Corner china cabinet with convex door panel; 32" wide, 20" deep, 58 1/2" high. In Pennsylvania, $1,500. ➔

Corner china cabinet with convex door panel; 29" wide, 17" deep, 63" high, 7 1/2" rail. In Illinois, $1,500. ⬅

China cabinet with convex glass in side panels, beveled mirror in the upper section of the inside, and paw feet; 50" wide, 15" deep, 63" high. In Indiana, $995.

China cabinet with convex glass in side panels, incised carving on back rail, and spade feet; 38" wide, 14" deep, 68" high. In Iowa, $795.

China cabinet with convex glass panels and scroll feet; 35" wide, 16" deep, 61" high. In Michigan, $795. →

China cabinet with three flat glass panels; 42" wide at back, 15" deep, 60" high. In Illinois, $875. ←

China cabinet with convex glass in side panels and in central door, and mirrors in back of the two top shelves; 39" wide, 16" deep, 70" high. In Kentucky, $1,150.

China cabinet with fumed oak finish and flat glass panels in the sides and door; 37" wide, 13" deep, 69" high. In Illinois, $945.

China cabinet with round column and paw feet, and three convex glass panels; 36" wide, 13" deep, 63" high. In Wisconsin, $975.

China cabinet with scroll pillars, a style called "colonial" in the catalogs of the 1920s; 44" wide, 14" deep, 51" high, $745.

Corner cupboard with chamfered stiles; 45" wide, 20" deep, 97" high - too high for most modern homes, $1,050.

→

China cabinet with convex glass in door and side panels and scroll feet; 44" wide, 17" deep, 64" high, $995.

←

DINING ROOM

*China cabinet;
40" wide, 12"
deep, 63" high,
$695.*

*China cabinet with beading across top, 39" wide,
13" deep, 49" high, $725.*

*Corner cup-
board with
glass panels
that were
originally
wooden; 36"
wide, 20"
deep, 89"
high, $1,150.*

*China cabinet with leaded glass at top of straight
glass doors: 40" wide, 13" deep, 60" high, $895.*

Corner cupboard; 51" wide, 18" deep, 85" high. In Illinois, $1,425.

China cabinet with applied wooden grillwork on glass; 41" wide, 16 1/4" deep, 63 1/2" high. In Pennsylvania, $995.

China cabinet with fretwork at top of flat glass doors and scroll feet; 40" wide, 13" deep, 58" high, $895.

China cabinet with glass shelves; 36" wide, 12" deep, 49" high. In Kentucky, $875.

China cabinet with convex glass on door and side panels; 42" wide, 16" deep, 62 1/2" high, 2" rail. In Iowa, $995.

China cabinet with convex glass in side panels, incised carving on back rail; 38" wide, 14" deep, 68" high. In Iowa, $795.

Corner china cabinet with concave glass door and straight glass side panels; 40 1/2" wide, 24" deep, 69 1/2" high. In Illinois, $1,500.

China cabinet and storage unit that was once a built-in unit; 70" wide, 21" deep, 92" high. In Iowa, $3,500.

Plate rail; 22" wide, 2" deep, 10" high. In Iowa, $195.

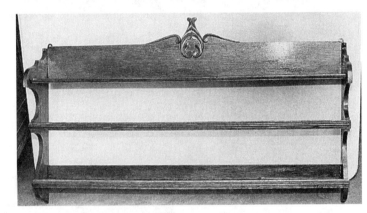

Plate rail; 36" wide, 5 1/2" deep, 20" high. In Iowa, $195.

Plate rail; 41" wide, 4" deep, 15" high. In Ohio, $245.

Plate rail; 38 1/2" wide, 4 1/2" deep, 14 1/2" high. In Illinois, $195.

Chapter 5

The Kitchen

The cook stove, often called a range, as well as cupboards and iceboxes, were integral kitchen furnishings in days of yore. A black cast-iron stove was fed wooden chips, corncobs, and coal or wood. Its heat was welcome on cold, winter days.

Mail order catalogs put out by various companies, most notably Wards and Sears, offered a tempting array of merchandise for the kitchen. A 1929 Montgomery Ward catalog still advertised the cast-iron range, but also pictured gas, oil, and kerosene burning ranges available in a variety of colors including spring green, French gray, ivory, and turquoise blue. Their lines were less bulky than the black kitchen stove, which was soon to become obsolete.

Before the built-in kitchen of today, our ancestors relied heavily on the Hoosier-type cabinet. Since Indiana is called the Hoosier State, it seemed natural that a manufacturer from New Castle, Indiana would choose to name his kitchen cabinet a Hoosier. This cabinet evolved from a baker's table, and had a flat work surface with pullout sliding boards, drawers for storing cutlery, and perhaps two bins. One of these bins was large enough to hold the flour supply, while the other was divided so that rye might be kept on one side and cornmeal on the other. Another alternative would find sugar in one side of the divided bin.

Someone decided that there was a great deal of space going to waste, so a top for spices, pans, dishes, or what-have-you was added to these tables. The baker's table expanded into a baker's cabinet.

Cooking time charts with weights and measures were included with the order of one of these cabinets. A metal-lined bread drawer contained holes for ventilation. Flour sifters were frequently present along with swing-out sugar jars. The work area was increased when a porcelain, zinc, or wooden work surface on which the upper section rested, could be pulled out.

The use of the name "Hoosier" spread until it became the generic title for all cupboards of this type manufactured in the early decades of the 1900s. The Sellers Company of Elwood, Indiana, romantically christened one of their models the "June Bride." Another version was so helpful it must have been able to replace the hired girl because it was called the "Kitchen Maid." Other Indiana producers of Hoosier cabinets included Ingram Richardson Manufacturing Company of Frankfort; Wasmuth Endicott Company of Andrews; McDougall of Frankfort; and Napanee Dutch Kitchinet of Napanee. These kitchen cupboards were also manufactured in other states. A Hawkeye cabinet was made in Burlington, Iowa. In Louisville, Kentucky, Scheirich and Company made such a cabinet, and Wilson of Grand Rapids, Michigan also produced Hoosier-style cabinets.

Until the introduction of the time payment plan, it was a financial burden for a family of the early 1900s to pay for one of these cabinets. With credit, it was possible to go into debt one day and meet the purchase price gradually over extended tomorrows. Advertisements might state, "For five dollars down, five dollars monthly, and a small interest fee, the cabinet could be in your home working for you as you pay for it." The advertisements urged buyers, "Don't wait. Order today."

A bargain kitchen cabinet in golden oak was offered in the 1929 Wards catalog for the cash price of $18.45, or an easy payment price of $20.45. Sears Roebuck, in its 1927 catalog, advertised a "Splendid Kitchen Cabinet" in a choice of five attractive finishes with the following prices: Golden Oak $34.65; White Enamel $36.85; Gray Enamel $36.95; Frosted Golden Brown Oak, Two-Tone $39.75 and Frosted Silver Gray Oak, Two-Tone $39.85.

A cabinet might include a slatted, flexible shutter or door that could be opened sideways (horizontally), or with an up or down pull (vertically). These flexible doors were made of thin strips of wood glued to a duck cloth or linen backing. Such closures, which operated in grooves, were called tambours. Occasionally, slag glass or amber panels added color to solid doors.

Other kitchen cupboards, which had glass enclosed doors at the top and drawers and solid doors at the base, were made more attractive by using incised or applied carvings. Ornamental cornices often crowned the top. These cabinets were available in step-back types where the bottom section protruded, and the top section was narrower than the base. Many, however, were one piece having straight up and down fronts.

When built-in cupboards became popular in the 1940s, Hoosiers became passé. For those who appreciated their nostalgia, Hoosiers became ornamental rather than utilitarian.

The icebox must have seemed like a precious treasure when it was introduced. In a chest version, the ice and food stood side by side in a metal-lined wooden box. In a refrigerator, air circulated constantly based on the principle that hot air rises. Warm air would hit the block of ice in the top, cool, and descend to the bottom. As it warmed, it rose again. The so-called oak icebox was often made of ash, elm, or other northern hardwoods.

Distributing ice was a summer season business, and many companies had horse and wagon carts delivering ice to city customers. Cards supplied by the companies were placed in a window. The cards indicated the amount of ice the household desired – twenty-five, fifty, seventy-five, or even one hundred pounds. Country people obtained ice through a do-it-yourself, cooperative effort. When streams froze in the winter, neighboring farmers banded together to cut ice. They marked off blocks and sawed along the lines to form huge cubes that they hauled away and stored until summer. At times, rundown vacant houses were filled with layers of ice insulated with a thick covering of sawdust or sand between the stacks. When a farmer needed ice, he picked up a block from this source. Ice picks or special shavers were used to chip small pieces of ice for cooling beverages.

The kitchen was a multi-purpose room. Besides being a cooking, eating, canning, and preserving site, it was the place where the family laundry and personal washing was done. Before pipes brought water into the house, all wastewater had to be dumped outside. A washbowl and pitcher were placed on a shelf or stand for quick cleanings before meals. A comb case of wood or tin, with an accompanying mirror, was often in this area, as was a hanging cabinet to hold shaving soap, a brush, and sharp-edged razors.

Traditionally, a washtub occupied the center of the floor on Saturday nights. Water heated on the stove was poured into the tub so each family member, in turn, could have a sit-down bath. On Monday, the housewife toted water from the well, heated it, and scrubbed the laundry in the kitchen, unless she had a separate washroom. She hung the wash outside over fences or on lines to dry, winter or summer.

Because of the presence of various types of tables that were found in the kitchen, particularly the drop leaf, this room also became a study and game room. Children could work on school projects at the table or enjoy a game. In cold months, the kitchen was a social center because it was usually the warmest room in the house. This comforting warmth was a calming influence when the youngsters of the house sat down on their highchairs for supper. Children's chair styles emulated those of their elders. Highchairs frequently had pressed designs on their backs. Ordinary highchairs from this era provided a safe place for a youngster to eat. They were available with or without tables (or trays, as they are more commonly called).

Spice cabinets with labels on the small drawers to identify various spices inside, were used in the kitchen when special seasonings, bought in hunk or seed form, were grated or pulverized at home. A mortar and pestle were used to grind or mash them when necessary. As the years passed, the identifying letters on these cabinets tended to fade. Even the words on metal nameplates could lose their readability after years of use.

Modern homemakers use these old spice cabinets in unique ways. They can hold sewing needs. When velvet liners are inserted in the drawers, the piece can become a jewelry holder. Vintage cabinets may retain a spicy odor. Signs of age, such as discoloration and bruised marks on the wood, should be present because these boxes are being reproduced today. If a spice box is desired for a special purpose, be sure to notice if it can rest flat as well as hang. Some spice cabinets have an extension at the base that does not permit them to be set down.

No kitchen of this time period would be complete without the presence of an oak wall telephone.

Alexander Graham Bell exhibited the original telephone design at the Centennial Exposition in Philadelphia in 1876. The public enjoyed the "toy" without expressing much interest. In 1877, a farsighted banker erected the first commercial telephone line, which extended three miles and connected his home with his bank in Boston. That same year a group of men founded what became the Bell Telephone Company. When some New York businesses first installed phones, they advertised the fact to indicate that they were progressive. Now such communication is not considered a novelty but a necessity.

In the beginning, boys were hired to operate telephone switchboards, but gradually women took over this task. Turning the crank on the old wooden phones caused "Central" (the operator) to answer, "Number, please." If someone were on your own party line, you could call direct, not by dialing, but by turning the crank. A long twist of the handle combined with short ones provided a calling system. A person's ring might be two longs and two shorts for example. Others on the line could quietly lift the receiver to eavesdrop, so neighbors were quick to know about the activities of others. Sometimes a third listener might interrupt and take over the conversation. It was never wise to gossip loosely on a party line.

Long wooden cases held the working parts of these wall telephones, and, in some rural areas, these were not removed from service until the late 1940s or early 1950s. A true collector likes to find a telephone with its works intact. Some old telephones are gutted to hold a modern telephone or radio. Others simply hang around as novelties or conversation pieces.

No wonder an unknown poet wrote this eulogy about the kitchen, "No matter where I seat my guests, they seem to like my kitchen best."

The icebox, usually made of oak or elm, was an integral part of the turn-of-the-century kitchen.

←

Hoosier-type kitchen cupboard with frosted doors, two wooden doors divided to slide open, and pullout work surface; 41" wide, 27" deep, 70" high. In Indiana, $995.

←

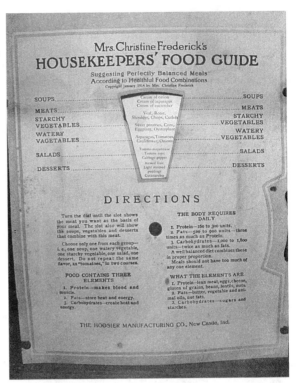

Hoosier kitchen cabinet, made in New Castle, Ind., with side moving tambour doors, porcelain pullout working surface, and an oval zinc label at the top reading "The Hoosier Saves Steps"; 42" wide, 25" deep, 71" high, $945.

The Housekeeper's Food Guide found inside the door of many Hoosier cabinets.

Hoosier-type kitchen cabinet with a pull-down tambour door, porcelain pullout working surface, and original floral designs on three doors with a plaque on front reading "Sellers Kitchen Cabinet, Elwood, Indiana"; 40" wide, 26" deep, 70" high, $945.

Hoosier-type kitchen cabinet, circa 1930s, with white factory finish, pull-down tambour door, porcelain pullout working surface, and a label reading "Ingram Richardson Mfg. Co., Frankfort, Ind."; 40" wide, 25" deep, 71" high, $625.

KITCHEN

A Cook Book Holder found inside a Hoosier-type cabinet marked "Napanee Dutch Kitchenet, pat. Feb. 24, 1914."

Metal holders for extras and other miscellaneous items found inside a Hoosier-type cabinet marked "Napanee Dutch Kitchenet, pat. Feb. 24, 1914."

Hoosier-type kitchen cabinet with three colored glass panels, pull-down tambour door, flour sifter, porcelain pullout working surface, and a label reading "Sellers The Better Kitchen Cabinet Kitchen Maid, Elwood, Ind., U.S.A. Trademark registered"; 41" wide, 27" deep, 70" high, $995.

Hoosier-type kitchen cabinet was used as an all-in-one unit for a baby. A quilted pad over porcelain pullout working surface was used for diaper changing, the flour bin housed the diapers, food was kept behind the pull-down tambour door, and other drawers held blankets and clothing; 40" wide, 27" deep, 69" high, $895.

KITCHEN

KITCHEN

Hoosier-type Kitchen cabinet with a pull-down tambour door and a pullout cutting board with breadboard ends; 40" wide, 24" deep, 69" high, $895.

Hoosier-type Kitchen cabinet with a pull-down tambour door, porcelain pullout working surface, metal breadbox and sifter, identified as "June Bride," manufactured by Sellers; 41" wide, 25" deep, 70" high, $895.

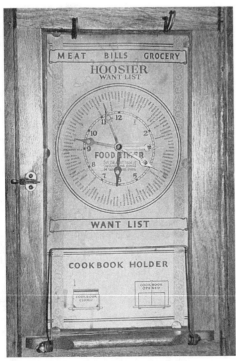

Sign found inside Hoosier cabinet.

Hoosier cabinet; 41" wide, 26 1/2" deep, 71" high. In Iowa, $995.

KITCHEN

Sellers cabinet; 47 1/2" wide, 26 1/2" deep, 81 1/4" high. In Iowa, $1,150.

Sellers cabinet; 40" wide, 28" deep, 70" high. In Iowa, $895.

Sellers cabinet; 40 1/2" wide, 27" deep, 70" high. In Illinois, $845.

Hoosier-type kitchen cabinet made in Andrews, Indiana, by the Wasmuth Endicott Co.; 40" wide, 29" deep, 71 1/4" high. In Iowa, $895.

Hoosier-type kitchen cabinet with tambour or folding door that goes up from porcelain instead of down from cabinet; 34" wide, 25" deep, 71" high. In Iowa, $795.

Boone kitchen cabinet; 37 1/2" wide, 23" deep, 71 1/4" high. In Iowa, $925.

Hoosier-type kitchen cabinet; 43" wide, 26" deep, 70 1/2" high. In Wisconsin, $925.

Greencastle kitchen cabinet; 42" wide, 28" deep, 67 1/2" high. In Illinois, $995

KITCHEN

KITCHEN

Kitchen cabinet from the 1930s with a metal plaque reading, "Scheirich, Louisville, Ky." and with the tambour pull-down missing; 40" wide, 26" deep, 71" high. In Kentucky, $775.

Kitchen cabinet, called by various names including "Bakers Cabinet," "Doughboy Cupboard" and "Possum Belly"; 43" wide, 27" deep, 71" high. In Indiana, $1,150.

Hoosier kitchen cabinet with tambour sliding doors and porcelain pull-out work area; 41" wide, 26" deep, 71" high. In Indiana, $925.

Kitchen cabinet with metal plaque reading, "Wilson Kitchen Cabinet, The Best"; 42" wide, 27" deep, 71" high. In Iowa, $945.

Hoosier kitchen cabinet dated 1910, with copper-plated original hardware and replaced porcelain knobs; 40" wide, 28" deep 68" high. In Iowa, $895.

Label found inside the top door of the Napanee Dutch Kitchenet.

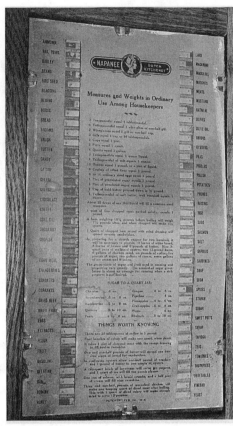

Napanee Dutch Kitchenet with tambour pull-down door and porcelain work surface, patented Feb. 24, 1914; 40" wide, 28" deep, 71" high. In Michigan, $895.

Kitchen cabinet with porcelain work surface, pull-down tambour door, and door pulls marked with an S to indicate it is a Sellers cabinet; 41" wide, 27" deep, 67" high. In Iowa, $895.

Kitchen cabinet patented March 14, 1916 with frosted glass panels in upper doors, tambour sliding doors, and original glasses and sugar container; 40" wide, 28" deep, 70" high. In Wisconsin, $945.

Kitchen cabinet with porcelain work surface, slag glass in top panels of upper doors and with a metal plaque reading, "Sellers, Elwood, Indiana"; 41" wide, 27" deep, 70" high. In Illinois, $895.

Kitchen cabinet marked "Wilson" on a metal plaque with slag glass in top panels of upper doors; the tambour pull-down is missing; 40" wide, 25" deep, 69" high. In Illinois, $875.

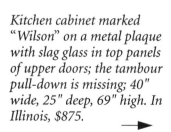

KITCHEN

Hoosier-type kitchen cabinet with tambour pull-down door and porcelain work surface; 42" wide, 25" deep, 66" high. In Illinois, $845.

Two-piece Hawkeye kitchen cabinet made by the Union Furniture Co., Burlington, Iowa; 47" wide, 28" deep, 81" high. In Illinois, $1,350.

Hoosier-type cupboard with sugar and flour bins and pullout cutting board; 42" wide, 26" deep, 73" high. In Illinois, $1,150.

←

KITCHEN

Elm kitchen cupboard; 40" wide, 17" deep, 68" high, $725.

An oak cupboard marriage with a base and top that were not originally together; 43" wide, 18" deep, 85" high, $825.

Kitchen cabinet; 42" wide, 24" deep, 77" high, $1,250.

Step-back kitchen cabinet with incised lines; 40" wide, 19" deep, 84" high, $845.

Oak-ash two-piece cupboard; 38" wide, 16 1/2" deep, 83" high. In Indiana, $945.

Two-piece step-back kitchen cabinet with incised lines; 40" wide, 19" deep, 84" high, $895.

Cupboard with dry sink and pullout work area; 50" wide, 30" deep, 78" high. In Michigan, $2,250.

Cupboard showing the pullout work area extended.

Ash kitchen desk cabinet with spoon carving on drawer and door fronts; 41" wide, 17" deep, 82" high. See next picture for view of writing area. In Illinois, $950.

Ash kitchen desk cabinet with drop-front writing area exposed.

Stepback cupboard; 36 1/2" wide, 16 1/2" deep, 83" high. In Iowa, $955.

Stepback cupboard; 43" wide, 18" deep, 89 1/2" high. In Iowa, $1,450.

Stepback cupboard with pie shelf; 41" wide, 17" deep, 91" high. In Iowa, $950.

Stepback cupboard with pie shelf; 38" wide, 16" deep, 80" high. In Illinois, $945.

Closed cupboard (without glass at top) with pie shelf; 43" wide, 16 1/2" deep, 84" high. In Indiana, $955.

Stepback cupboard with pie shelf; 40" wide, 12" deep, at top and 16 at base, 78" high. In Michigan, $1,150.

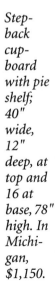

Stepback cupboard with applied decorations; 39" wide, 22" deep, 87" high. In Illinois, $995.

Kitchen cabinet with galvanized work area; 48" wide, 26" deep, 79" high. In Illinois, $995.

Hoosier-type kitchen cabinet with two small, round bottom-drawer bins and two pull-out bread boards; 45" wide, 26" deep at base, 12" deep at top, 78" high. In Illinois, $1,150.

Two-piece kitchen cupboard (a marriage of an elm top and oak bottom); 44" wide, 79" high. In Iowa, $975.

KITCHEN

KITCHEN

Step-back cupboard; 40" wide, 19" deep, 74" high. In Illinois, $945.

Step-back cupboard; 39" wide, 20" deep at the base, 82" high. In Indiana, $945.

Step-back cupboard with applied decorations on cornice; 47" wide, 24" deep, 85" high. In Wisconsin, $1,150.

Open cupboard with pie shelf; 43" wide, 26" deep, 74" high. In Wisconsin, $855.

Dry sink cabinet with pullout dough board supported by attached leg; 52" wide, 30" deep, 70" high. In Indiana, $1,650.

Two-piece open step-back cupboard with pie shelf and work area between the two parts; 46" wide, 26" deep, 71" high. In Wisconsin, $995.

Baker's cabinet; 42" wide, 28 1/2" deep at the base, 11" deep at top section, 63" high. In Illinois, $1,150.

Ash kitchen cupboard with spoon carving and incised lines; 40" wide, 17" deep, 82" high. $795.

One-piece kitchen cabinet with glass doors in upper section; 37" wide, 16" deep, 73" high, $895.

One-piece kitchen cabinet with glass doors in upper section; 36" wide, 14" deep, 74" high, $895.

Kitchen cabinet with straight front and pressed designs on drawers and doors; 40" wide, 16" deep, 77" high. In Illinois, $855.

Straight front cupboard; 36 1/2" wide, 16 1/2" deep, 72" high. In Illinois, $795.

Straight-front cupboard with incised, spooncarved, and applied decorations; 28" wide, 14" deep, 78" high. In Wisconsin, $1,295.

Straight-front cupboard with applied decorations on cornice; 37" wide, 15" deep, 83" high. In Michigan, $945.

Straight-front cupboard; 38" wide, 16" deep, 72" high. In Illinois, $895.

Cupboard with base that slants out at the bottom: 39" wide, 15" deep at top and 20" at base, 70" high. In Michigan, $995.

Late 1800s corner cupboard with two drawers and two doors; 40" wide, 23" deep, 78" high. In Michigan, $1,750.

Breadboard resembles desk, but raised rolltop reveals pullout breadboard; 32 1/2" wide, 21" deep, 60" high. In Iowa, $1,450.

Kitchen cabinet with cylinder front that covers a pullout doughboard; 33" wide, 21" deep, 64" high. In Illinois, $1,250.

An oak pie safe marriage with added splash back and drawers; 45" wide, 15" deep, 57" to top surface, $895.

Pie safe with six pierced-tin panels; 41" wide, 15" deep, 56" high. In Illinois, $695.

Plain-sawed oak jelly cupboard; 41" wide, 17" deep, 54" high. In Iowa, $695.

→

Ash drop-leaf table; 41" by 23", 29" high with 15" drop leaves, $295.

Kitchen worktable, dated Jan. 6, 1941 in drawer; 42" wide, 25" deep, 30" high, $345.

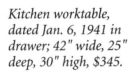

Oval drop-leaf table; 41" by 22", 31" high, 13" drop leaves, $395.

Drop-leaf extension table with two 12" leaves; 29" by 43", 30" high, 13" drop leaves, with four accompanying chairs that are not pictured. $655 for the set.

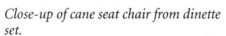
Dinette table with splayed legs - 30" square, 30" high; cane seat, splatback chairs - 38" high. In Iowa, table $440; chairs $195 each.

Close-up of cane seat chair from dinette set.

KITCHEN

Tavern table with four compartments to hold beverages so the top surface remains free for card playing; 40" wide, 30" deep, 31" high, $695.

Drop-leaf extension table, 42" x 26", with one drop leaf in down position; 30" high. In Illinois, $325.

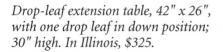

1920-era dinette extension table - 48" x 36", 30" high. In Illinois, table $245; pair of chairs, $115.

Dinette or breakfast set with quarter-sawed oak drop-leaf table and two Windsor-style chairs from the 1920s; table 32" x 24", 31" high with two 11" drop leaves; chairs, 36" high. In Iowa, $325 for the set.

Splay-legged tavern table from the 1930s or 1940s with beverage holders at each corner; 39" wide, 33" deep, 30" high. In Wisconsin, $515.

Bent-back kitchen chair with bent parts of hickory or elm; 36" high, set of 4, $145 each.

Dinette table from Depression era; 30" square, 30" high. In Michigan, $295.

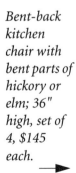

Icebox, currently in use, with a label reading "Lapland Monitor, The Ramey Refrigerator Co., Greenville, Mich."; 35" wide, 20" deep, 48" high. $625.

Icebox with zinc interior intact; 26" wide, 19" deep, 48" high, $695.

Icebox with a label reading "American House Furniture Co."; 21" wide, 14" deep, 37" high, $695.

Icebox with lift lid for ice compartment, molded panels, and a label reading "Cold Storage"; 28" wide, 17" deep, 43" high, $695.

Icebox with brass plaque reading "New Iceberg" and lift-lid ice compartment; 31" wide, 21" deep, 45" high. In Iowa, $850.

Ash icebox; 30" wide, 18" deep, 48" high. In Illinois, $695.

Ash icebox, patented June 30, 1925, with brass plaque reading, "A Life Preserver for Food"; 21" wide, 16" deep, 48" high. In Iowa, $545.

Buffalo icebox; 29" wide, 19" deep, 42 1/2" high. In Maryland, $795.

Lorraine icebox made in LaCrosse, Wisconsin, by LaCrosse Refrig. Corp.; 31" wide, 15" deep, 42" high. In Illinois, $645.

Icebox with Estey Royale brass plaque that is not original; 25" wide, 18" deep, 38" high. In Ohio, $645.

Icebox; 32" wide, 22" deep, 41" high. In Illinois, $695.

Icebox; 35" wide, 18" deep, 39" high. In Illinois, $525.

KITCHEN

Double-door icebox with metal label reading, "North Pole"; 25" wide, 19" deep, 55" high. In Wisconsin, $625.

Icebox marked with a metal plaque, "Victor, Challenge Refrigerator Co., Grand Haven, Mich. U.S.A." 22" wide, 15" deep, 40" high. In Iowa, $565.

Icebox with brass plaque reading, "Success Huenefeld Co., Cincinnati, Ohio"; 26" wide, 18" deep, 43" high. In Indiana, $745.

Medicine chest; 17" wide, 6" deep, 28" high, $245.

Medicine chest; 15" wide, 6" deep, 19" high, $235.

KITCHEN

Medicine cabinet with towel rack, often found in the kitchen, held shaving paraphernalia as well as medicinal supplies; 18" wide, 5 1/2" deep, 22" high. In Illinois, $225.

Comb case with spoon carving on front of base; 11 1/4" wide, 15" high. In Iowa, $175.

Wall pocket or comb case; 13" wide, 3" deep, 10" high. In Iowa, $145.

Medicine cabinet; 19" wide, 6" deep, 23 1/4" high. In Illinois, $245.

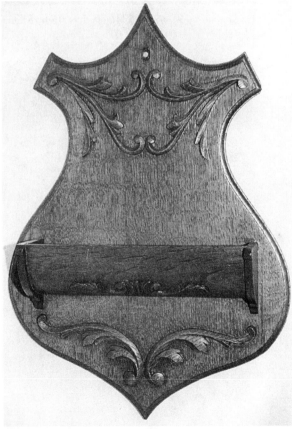

Comb case; 11" wide, 3" deep, 15" high. In Iowa, $195.

Comb case with mirror and incised decorations; 14" wide, 4" deep, 24" high. In Colorado, $195.

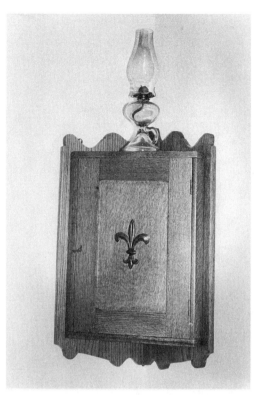

Hanging corner cabinet; 18 1/2" wide, 8 1/2" deep, 26" high. In Colorado, $275.

Medicine cabinet; 17" wide, 7" deep, 18" high, 4 1/2" back rail. In Wisconsin, $215.

Medicine cabinet; 16" wide, 6" deep, 27" high. In Michigan, $245.

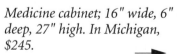

Spice box, $225.

Spice cabinet; 10" wide, 5" deep, 17" high. In Iowa, $255.

Spice cabinet; 11" wide, 5 1/2" deep, 17 1/2" high. In Wisconsin, $255.

Spice cabinet; 11" wide, 5" deep, 13 1/2" high. In Illinois, $255.

Spice cabinet; 10" wide, 5" deep, 16" high. In Iowa, $225.

←

KITCHEN

Revolving spice dispenser made by the G.E. Stewart Co., Mfgrs., Norwalk, Ohio, patented June 20, 1901 and supplied by them to McFadden Coffee & Spice Co., Dubuque, Iowa (the other side holds ginger, mustard, and pepper); 14 1/2" wide, 8" deep, 29" high. In Wisconsin, $295.

KITCHEN

Wall telephone made by Stromberg Carlson; 9" wide, 6" deep, 18" high, $310.

Wall telephone made by Eureka Electric Co., Chicago; 12" wide, 32" high, $345.

Wall telephone made by Kellogg, Chicago, and patented Nov. 26, 1901; 11" wide, 6" deep, 23" high, $310.

Wall telephone; 8 1/2" wide, 18" high. In Illinois, $310.

Wall telephone. In Ohio, $395.

Wall telephone. In Wisconsin, $325.

Wall telephone. In Wisconsin, $325.
→

KITCHEN

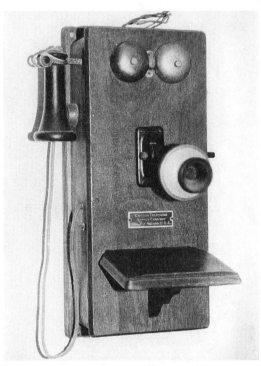

Wall telephone made by Chicago Telephone Supply Company of Elkhart, Indiana. In Iowa, $325.

Monarch wall telephone; 9" wide, 6" deep, 26" high. In Wisconsin, $345.

Wall telephone; 8" wide, 6" deep, 24" high. In Wisconsin, $345.

←

Chapter 6

The Children's Room

Pint sized furniture for little ones has a special quality that attracts adult attention. Sometimes, a question arises in an owner's mind. Is the miniature a salesman's sample or a child's possession? The draw table pictured in this section (p. 136) could be either. However, its knowledgeable owner labels it the former.

Many women enjoy collecting nostalgic childhood items. Perhaps it helps them recall happy hours of yore when they sat in small rockers and pretended to put their baby dolls to sleep. People often visit antique shows and shops in search of items that remind them of their childhood.

Children's furniture includes both items intended for play and items intended for more practical use. Play items include doll beds, doll dressers, and doll cupboards. Practical items include highchairs, cradles, rockers, desks, and chiffoniers.

Patented furniture was a vital part of the late 1800s industrial development. Beds folded into desks, chests, or wardrobes, while chairs rocked on all types of platforms or jolted on springs. Highchairs could confuse baby by collapsing into a stroller or bed. Look for patent dates on any mechanical furniture; the piece was fashioned sometime after the last patent listed.

Some highchairs have wheels and can be folded down into "go-carts." A child was then free to wheel about the room with ease. When raised again, the high chair returned. These chairs command a higher price than plainer examples. A combination rocking highchair is another out-of-the-ordinary type. It can be used either in the upright position or collapsed down into a rocking chair. Highchairs with T-backs, so named because the back resembles the letter "T," are readily available. One of the photographs in this chapter shows a signed Thonet bentwood highchair. Michael Thonet created bentwood furniture in Vienna, Austria around 1840. Soon this style was being successfully mass-produced. Its designer felt that it was strong, functional, and aesthetically pleasing.

At times, trays were removed from a highchair so an older child could be pushed up to the table to eat. The chair then resembled what is known as a youthchair. A bow-back youth chair with arms had legs that splay out. A flamingo decorates the back of one unusual pressed and carved youth chair pictured in this chapter (p. 132).

Child-sized old-time desks are also available. Most desks were made in styles resembling those of adult desks. Some have lift-lids; others are of the combination bookcase type. Generally, unusual desks are more costly. A drop-lid desk, with applied decorations on its lid and floral designs cut out on its side, is attractive. Dainty roll top desks can also be found. A 26-inch high flat back chair was often used with a small desk.

Rockers for little ones can have cane seats and pressed designs on their backs. Some versions are copies of the stern, straight Mission-style and are sought by those who collect Mission furniture.

Collectors eagerly seek doll dressers. Child's chiffoniers with swing mirrors are difficult to find, and it is possible that they may be father- or grandfather-made creations.

A child's one-piece straight lined kitchen cabinet with glass doors at the top and solid wood doors and drawers at the base was fun for girls to put their doll dishes in, as they played house.

Pressed-back cane seat highchair go-cart combination; 17" wide, 19" deep, 41" high. $645.

Highchair converted into youth chair; 41" high. $245. ➤

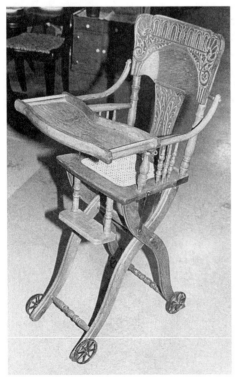

Cane seat highchair go-cart combination; 42" high. $595.

Pressed-back cane seat highchair; 42" high. $445.

⬅

Highchair with T-back and splayed legs; 18" wide, 39" high. $395.

Bow-back youth chair; 14" arm to arm. 38" high. In Iowa, $225.

Veneer-back youth chair; 14" arm to arm, 40" high. In Iowa, $225.

Highchair with table or tray; 40 1/2" high. In Ohio, $255.

Pressed-back highchair with cane seat and table or tray; 43 1/2" high. In Illinois, $495.

Pressed-back highchair with table or tray; 40 1/2" high. In Iowa. $285.

Cane seat youth chair with pressed/ carved-back flamingo decoration; 42" high. In Iowa, $295.

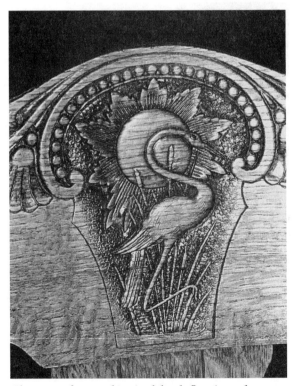

Close-up of pressed/carved-back flamingo decoration on youth chair.

Cane seat highchair/go-cart combination with table or tray; 40" high. In Iowa, $545.
←

Cane seat highchair/go-cart combination with table or tray and pressed pineapple slats; 40" high. In Iowa, $565.

Cane seat and back highchair/go-cart combination with table or tray missing; in down position, 13 1/2" wide, 16 1/2" deep, 24" high. In Illinois. $285.

Cane back and seat bentwood highchair, signed "Thonet"; 16" wide at tray, 37" high. In Iowa, $445. →

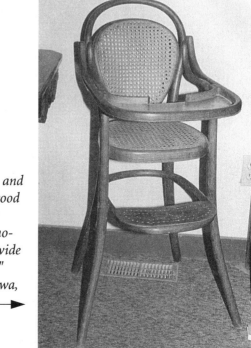

Rocking highchair; 17 1/4" wide, 40" high. In Michigan, $565.

Rocking highchair shown in down or rocking position.

Cane seat single pressed-back highchair/ go-cart combination, marked Wait Chair Co., 1903; 41" high. In Wisconsin, $545.

←

Highchair/go-cart combination; 37" high. In Iowa, $565.

→

T-back highchair; 18" arm to arm, 19" deep, 39" high. In Wisconsin, $295.

Highchair/go-cart combination with pressed-cane seat and pressed design on back and splat; 18" wide, 38" high. In Wisconsin, $555.

Cane-seat Mother Goose pressed-back highchair; 42" high. In Wisconsin. $295.

Close-up of Mother Goose pressed back.

Child's drop-lid desk with applied decorations and flower cutouts on the sides; 22" wide, 11" deep, 33" high. $345.

Child's C-curve rolltop desk; 26" wide, 16" deep, 37" high. $345.

Draw table that could have been an apprentice's piece, a salesman's sample, or a child's table; 26" wide, 16" deep, 22" high, 8" draw leaves. $455.

Child's lift-lid desk; 27" wide, 18" deep, 35" high. In Iowa, $385.

Child's combination bookcase-desk with desk on left-hand side to accommodate left-handed writer; 38" wide, 11" deep, 47" high. In Iowa, $845.

Child's combination bookcase-desk with desk on left-hand side to accommodate left-handed writer; 32" wide, 13" deep, 56" high. In Illinois, $875.

Child's fall-front desk with French-style legs and ribbon decoration on drop lid; 19" wide, 13 1/2" deep, 39" high. In Wisconsin, $415.

Child's C-curve rolltop desk; 33" wide, 21" deep, 41" high. In Michigan, $515.

Child's C-rolltop desk; 24" wide, 17" deep, 35" high. In Illinois. $315.

Quarter-sawed oak child's rocker with rolled seat and veneered back; 15" arm to arm, 24" high. $185.

Child's pressed-back rocker; 28" high. $265.

Child's rocker; 28" high. $195.

Child's pressed-back rocker; 28" high. $195.

CHILDREN'S ROOM

Child's rocker; 21" arm to arm, 29" high. $195.

Child's plank seat rocker; 29" high. In Illinois, $195.

Child's cane seat pressed-back rocker with twisted spindles; 15 1/2" arm to arm, 28" high. $285.

Child's pressed-back rocker with pressed design on splat, made by Stomps Burkhardt Co., Dayton, Ohio; 21" arm to arm, 32" high. In Indiana, $295.

Child's mission rocker; 26" high. $215.

Child's slat-back chair that could be used with child's desk; 26" high. $115.

Elm and maple youth chair, 44" high. In Michigan, $165.

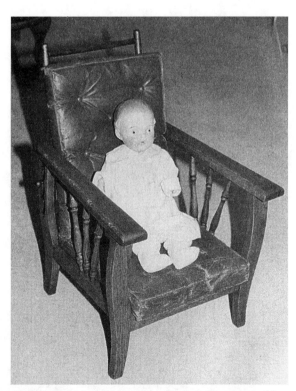

Child's Morris-style recliner chair with a movable metal rod that controls the reclining angle; 18" arm to arm, 26" high. In Wisconsin. $345.

CHILDREN'S ROOM

Cradle on platform; 21" wide, 39" long, 33" high. $495.

Cradle on platform with applied decorations; 23" wide, 42" long, 46" high. $795.

Baby bed; 22" wide, 39" long, 25" high. $445.

Doll bed with pressed design in head- and footboards; 12 1/2" wide, 24 1/2" long, 15" high at headboard, 9 1/4" high at footboard. In Wisconsin, $175.

CHILDREN'S ROOM

Ash and selected hardwood cradle; 38" wide, 22" deep, 31" high. In Michigan, $525.

Child's chiffonier or chest of drawers with swing mirror; 22" wide, 15" deep, 58" high. $645.

Child's one-piece kitchen cabinet; 22" wide, 11" deep, 40" high. $745.

Child's ash doll dresser; 13 1/2" wide, 7" deep, 26 1/2" high. In Wisconsin, $255.

Child's chiffonier with swing mirror; 22" wide, 13" deep, 30" to chiffonier top, 16 1/2" high mirror. In Iowa, $695.

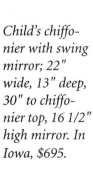

Child's chiffonier with swing mirror; 22" wide, 13" deep, 30" to chiffonier top, 16 1/2" high mirror. In Illinois, $600.

Child's doll cupboard; 7 1/2" wide, 4" deep, 9 1/2" high, 1 1/2" back rail. In Illinois, $165.

CHILDREN'S ROOM

Child's doll dresser; 12 1/2" wide, 6 1/2" deep, 11" high. In Illinois, $185.

Child's doll dresser; 14" wide, 7" deep, 14 1/4" high. In Iowa, $295.

CHILDREN'S ROOM

Child's plant stand; 11 1/2" square, 19 1/2" high. In Illinois, $155.

←

Child's "Teddy" wagon with orange spoke wheels and slats that form its bed; 14" wide, 36" deep. $545. →

Chapter 7

The Library

The home library, from the late 1800s through the early 1900s, would normally house the following pieces of furniture — chairs, desks, bookcases, library tables, and filing cabinets. Also included in this chapter are music boxes, organs, and phonographs. Only the homes of the wealthy had separate areas reserved for musical activities. The library can be considered somewhat equivalent to the home office of today.

One desk in style during this Golden Oak period was the combination bookcase desk. This unit had a fall front or drop lid, storage drawers or doors beneath, and a glass enclosure for books. Frequently, convex glass panels kept the contents of the bookcase dust free. In others, a flat sheet of glass was used for this purpose.

Built-in beveled mirrors, shelves for decorative items, incised and applied carvings, bracket, scroll, or paw feet are some embellishments that enhance these desks. In most cases, the desks are built to accommodate a right-handed user as the writing surface is on the right side of the desk. Several examples in this chapter picture the less commonly found desks for those who are left-handed. A desk built for the ambidextrous writer has a bookcase on each side of the fall front.

An unusual fall front with enclosed storage space beneath the desk features a beveled mirror flanked by two grotesques. It is called a Sheboygan desk. These grotesque carvings have animal bodies and fish tails.

Simpler desks, known as fall-front parlor desks or lady's desks, have drop lids over a single or double drawer. Many are embellished with applied decorations and incised carvings.

Secretaries are tall units, consisting of a desk with drawers or doors beneath the writing surface and a bookcase on top. Another style of secretary has a cylinder front. Many of these desks were manufactured in the furniture capitol of the United States, Grand Rapids, Michigan.

The Phoenix Furniture Company of Grand Rapids manufactured a "French Cylinder" desk which they described as unique. A sliding lid closed down over the writing surface and its pigeonholes. Its seventeen drawers could be locked with one key.

In popularity, roll-top desks rank high. Two types of roll-top desks, the S-curve and the C-curve, are available. When these desks are cluttered, the roll top can be pulled down to hide the debris. Often used in conjunction with these desks are swivel desk or office chairs.

Originally designed to store books, bookcases today are often used as a place to display collectible and antique fine china and glass.

Sectional or stack bookcases were common during the Golden Oak period. They could have decorative tops and bases as well as a series of glass doors that pulled open and slid in to permit a user to take out or put away a desired volume. Often leaded glass enhanced the more expensive cases. This type of bookcase could grow in number, by adding sections, as the family library expanded.

The Gunn Company of Grand Rapids, Michigan made one such bookcase in 1899. Others were made by Globe-Wernicke of Cincinnati, Ohio and by Macey of Grand Rapids, Michigan. In 1902, Sears offered a Bauch extension bookcase that could be shipped knocked down to save freight expenses. Its glass doors, which slid on roller bearings for easy operation, enabled the book titles to be easily seen. Sections of these bookcases could be purchased in single or multiple units.

Library tables are common. These were available in a variety of styles and held books, periodicals and newspapers.

Odd as it may seem, old file cabinets are often used today by the younger generations to house VCR tapes and cassettes.

Combination bookcase-desk with frosted designs on convex door panel, projection drawer, applied decorations and paw feet; 37" wide, 11" deep, 71" high. In Wisconsin, $975.

Combination bookcase-desk with incised carving; 39" wide, 14" deep, 67" high, $995.

Combination bookcase-desk; 38" wide, 14" deep, 65" high, $795.

Combination bookcase-desk with convex glass door panel, projection swell drawer and applied decorations; 37" wide, 12" deep, 68" high, $895.

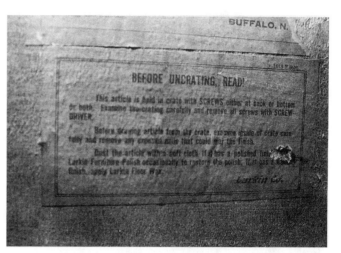

Label found on the back of the Larkin combination bookcase-desk.

Combination bookcase-desk supplied by Larkin Company; 42" wide, 14" deep, 67" high, $1,650.

Combination bookcase-desk with applied decorations and incised carving; 39" wide, 13" deep, 68" high, $845.

Combination bookcase-desk with convex glass door panel, applied decorations, and hood over desk area; 42" wide, 13" deep, 76" high, $2,050.

Combination bookcase-desk with incised decorations; 38" wide, 12" deep, 67" high, $1,150.

Combination bookcase-desk with convex glass door panel, leaded glass door over drop lid, pillar stiles, paw feet, and a label on the back reading "Factory #13, Larkin Co., Buffalo, N.Y. - Mr. C. Johnson to Moline, Illinois." $1,745.

Combination left-handed-style bookcase-desk with incised and applied decorations and swing mirror; 46" wide, 14" deep, 73" high, $1,050.

Combination left-handed-style bookcase-desk with incised decorations; 41" wide, 12" deep, 73" high, $1,150.

Combination bookcase-desk with applied decorations; 43" wide, 13" deep, 75" high, $895.

Combination bookcase-desk with etched designs on convex glass door front, two mirrors and applied decorations; 37" wide, 12" deep, 75" high. In Iowa, $1,350.

Combination bookcase-desk; 37" wide, 12" deep, 71" high. In Illinois, $1,050.

Combination bookcase-desk; 42" wide, 13" deep, 68 1/2" high. In Illinois, $995.

Combination bookcase-desk with convex bookcase door, leaded glass above drop front, applied decoration on top rail and paw feet; 42" wide, 14" deep, 76" high. In Iowa, $1,750.

Combination bookcase-desk; 37" wide, 13" deep, 76" high. In Iowa, $1,050.

Combination bookcase-desk with "open book" appearance of drop lid, and drawer above writing area; 42 1/2" wide, 13" deep, 67 1/2" high. In Iowa, $995.

Combination bookcase-desk with unusual convex-glass-enclosed storage compartment above writing area; 41 1/2" wide, 13 1/2" deep, 68" high. In Iowa, $1,525.

Combination bookcase-desk; 37" wide, 14" deep, 72" high. In Wisconsin, $955.

Combination bookcase-desk with flat-glass door front and applied decorations; 38" wide, 14" deep, 74" high. In Iowa, $1,150.

LIBRARY

Combination bookcase-desk with desk on left-hand side to accommodate a left-handed writer (the majority of combination desks have the desk section on the right-hand side); 43" wide, 14" deep, 72" high. In Illinois, $1,250.

Combination bookcase-desk with desk on the left-hand side to accommodate a left-handed writer; 41 1/2" wide, 13 1/2" deep, 72" high. In Illinois, $1,525.

Sheboygan desk with grotesques flanking mirror; 31 1/2" wide, 13 1/2" deep, 72" high. In Wisconsin, $1,575.

Close-up of grotesque that serves as mirror support on Sheboygan desk.

Combination bookcase-desk from the P.T. Barnum estate; 55 1/2" wide, 15" deep, 78 1/2" high. In Colorado, $2,250.

Quarter-sawed oak combination bookcase-desk with convex glass door and swell front top drawer; 37" wide, 12" deep, 70" high. In Wisconsin, $1,075.

Larkin combination bookcase-desk with original label on the back; 40" wide, 14" deep, 73" high. In Iowa, $995.

The same Larkin combination bookcase-desk, shown in the previous picture, after it was refinished. In Iowa, $1,250.

Combination wardrobe and desk with full length beveled mirror on wardrobe door, and desk with mirror and fall front; 52" wide, 13" deep, 77" high. In Kentucky, $1,250.

Combination bookcase-desk with convex glass door, beveled-glass mirror, applied decorations, swell drawer beneath drop lid, and paw feet; 38" wide, 12" deep, 69" high. In Iowa, $1,250.

Combination double bookcase-desk with convex glass doors, swell drawer beneath drop lid, and pressed decorations; 54" wide, 13" deep, 74" high. In Indiana, $1,575.

Combination bookcase-desk with applied decorations on drop lid and base door; 47" wide, 13" deep, 74" high. In Michigan, $995.

Combination bookcase-desk with applied decorations, leaded glass on top panel, and fretwork designs; 39" wide, 12" deep, 71" high. In Indiana, $895.

Combination bookcase-desk; 45" wide, 13" deep, 68" high. In Iowa, $875.

Fall-front desk with beveled mirrors, applied decorations, grotesque heads above shelf supports, swell drawers, and storage compartment with glass doors; 31" wide, 15" deep, 63" high. In Illinois, $1,150.

Quarter-sawed oak fall-front desk with bookcase at top; 35" wide, 13" deep, 63" high. In Iowa, $995.

Combination double bookcase-desk with convex glass doors, beveled mirror, applied decorations, and grotesque above mirror; 55" wide, 13" deep, 73" high. In Indiana, $1,750.

Combination bookcase-desk with beveled mirror and applied decorations; 45" wide, 14" deep, 75" high. In Wisconsin, $1,395.

Combination bookcase-desk with beveled mirror and applied decorations; 38" wide, 12" deep, 68" high. In Illinois, $895.

Combination bookcase-desk with convex glass door, beveled mirror, applied decorations, pressed carving, and paw feet; 36" wide, 11" deep, 71" high. In Illinois, $995.

Fall-front desk with applied decorations and double-door storage compartment beneath fall-front; 32" wide, 14" deep, 45" high. In Wisconsin, $875.

Fall-front parlor desk with storage compartments above and beneath drop lid; 28" wide, 15" deep, 62" high. In Iowa, $875. →

Combination bookcase-desk with convex glass door, beveled mirror, swell drawer beneath drop lid, applied decorations, and pressed carving; 37" wide, 11" deep, 72" high. In Wisconsin, $1,150.

Combination bookcase-desk with convex glass door, and applied decorations; 37" wide, 11" deep, 71" high. In Iowa, $945.

Grotesque on the cornice of a combination bookcase-desk.

Grotesque on fall front of a combination bookcase-desk.

Grotesque used as a shelf support on a combination bookcase-desk.

Grotesque applied to the pilaster in the bookcase section of a combination bookcase-desk.

Grotesque on desk fall front.

Fall-front parlor or lady's desk with applied deco-rations; 25" wide, 12" deep, 42" high, $795.

Lady's or parlor fall-front desk with one drawer, door and two shelves above drop lid; one drawer and two shelves below; and applied and incised decorations; 30" wide, 17" deep, 60" high. In Ohio, $1,650.

Fall-front desk that was originally a part of a side-by-side or combina-tion bookcase, with pressed designs; 22" wide, 14" deep, 41" high, $595.

←

Fall-front parlor desk with swell drawer fronts; 30" wide, 17" deep, 50" high, $875.

Fall-front parlor desk with serpentine lid, applied decorations and grotesque figure; 30" wide, 17" deep, 42" high, $645.

Fall-front parlor or lady's desk with swell drawer and applied decorations; 26" wide, 14" deep, 48" high, $595.

Fall-front desk with applied decorations and a metal rail; 26" wide, 17" deep, 38" high, $645.

Fall-front parlor desk; 27" wide, 14" deep, 42" high. In Iowa, $675.

LIBRARY

Fall-front parlor desk with applied decorations, mirror and provisions for books below; 30" wide, 12" deep, 62" high. In Iowa, $795.

Fall-front parlor desk; 27" wide, 13" deep, 64" high. In Michigan, $745.

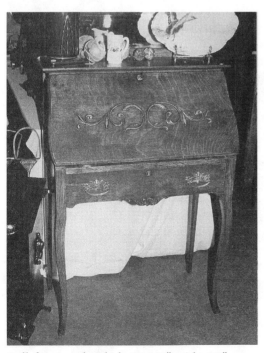

Fall-front parlor desk; 29 1/2" wide, 15" deep, 50" high. In Illinois, $495.

Fall-front desk; 33" wide, 12" deep, 62" high. In Illinois, $995.

LIBRARY

Fall-front parlor desk; 27 1/2" wide, 14" deep, 42" high. In Iowa, $645.

Fall-front parlor desk. The back is finished to resemble front with a fake fall front and drawer; 26 1/2" wide, 16 1/2" deep, 52 1/2" high. In Iowa, $895.

Fall-front table desk resembles the walnut Victorian style circa 1860; 36" wide, 24" deep, 58" high. In Pennsylvania, $945.

Fall-front parlor desk with incised and applied decorations and mirror on back rail; 29" wide, 14" deep, 58" high. In Iowa, $945.

Fall-front parlor desk with applied decorations and oval beveled mirror; 30" wide, 15" deep, 55" high. In Illinois, $795.

Fall-front desk with bureau base; 31" wide, 16" deep, 46" high. In Iowa, $845.

Fall-front desk with concave top drawers, beading, and applied decorations; 29" wide, 18" deep, 44" high. In Iowa, $595.

Fall-front desk with table base; 38" wide, 23" deep, 52" high. In Illinois, $795.

Ornately carved fall-front desk with Man-of-the-Wind designs on drop lid and drawer fronts; 36" wide, 24" deep, 49" high. In Illinois, $1,575.

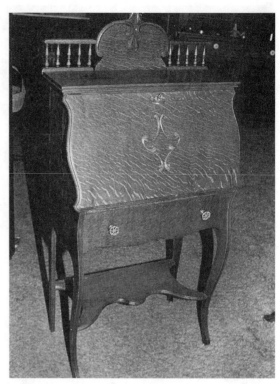

Lady's or parlor fall-front desk with applied decorations; 26" wide, 14" deep, 50" high. In Indiana, $395.

Fall-front parlor desk with two glass doors at top and scroll legs; 29" wide, 15" deep, 57" high. In Michigan, $725.

Quarter-sawed oak fall-front parlor desk; 32" wide, 16" deep, 47" high. In Kentucky, $645.

Fall-front lady's desk with beveled mirror and applied decorations; 30" wide, 17" deep, 51" high. In Illinois, $650.

Fall-front desk; 30" wide, 17" deep, 27" high. In Wisconsin, $595 including chair.

Fall-front desk with open storage space above lower drawer; 28" wide, 15" deep, 40" high. In Iowa, $625.

Fall-front desk; 30" wide, 17" deep, 25" high. In Wisconsin, $575.

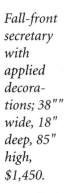

Fall-front secretary with applied decorations; 38"" wide, 18" deep, 85" high, $1,450.

→

Ash two-piece cylinder secretary with burl walnut on cylinder front and incised decorations; 24" wide, 21" deep, 91" high. In Iowa, $3,250.

Cylinder secretary with applied carving; 38" wide, 22" deep, 85" high, $2,150.

Fall-front secretary with applied decorations; 42" wide, 19" deep, 81" high. In Iowa, $1,450.

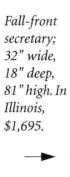

Fall-front secretary; 32" wide, 18" deep, 81" high. In Illinois, $1,695.

Fall-front secretary; 30" wide, 16" deep, 84" high. In Wisconsin, $1,650.

Fall-front secretary; 36" wide, 16" deep, 86" high. In Iowa, $1,795.

Fall-front secretary; 42" wide, 19" deep, 82" high. In Wisconsin, $2,225.

Cylinder front secretary; 38" wide, 22" deep, 90 1/2" high. In Iowa, $2,450.

Ash fall-front secretary; 36" wide, 18" deep, 85" high. In Wisconsin, $1,895.

Cylinder secretary with incised lines and applied decorations; 42" wide, 23" deep, 91" high. In Iowa, $3,495.

Ash fall-front secretary with applied decorations and beading; 36" wide, 19" deep, 85" high. In Iowa, $1,950.

Fall-front secretary with incised and applied decorations; 35" wide, 18" deep, 78" high. In Illinois, $1,125.

Quarter-sawed oak fall-front desk with bookcase at top; 35" wide, 13" deep, 63" high. In Iowa, $995.

Plantation-type desk with bird's-eye maple door panels; 36" wide, 27" deep, 72" high. In Kentucky, $875.

←

LIBRARY

S-curve rolltop desk with finished back; 54" wide, 30" deep, 46" high. In Illinois, $1,650.

Quarter-sawed oak S-curved rolltop desk; 55" wide, 36" deep, 46" high, $3,800.

S-curve rolltop desk and another roll on the left side of the kneehole with a pullout shelf; 55" wide, 34" deep, 53" high, $2,500.

S-curve rolltop desk; 48" wide, 31" deep, 48" high, $1,950.

S-curve rolltop desk; 46" wide, 36" deep, 46" high, $4,250.

S-curve rolltop desk; 50" wide, 34" deep, 46" high, $2,400.

C-curve rolltop desk; 36" wide, 28" deep, 44" high, $875.

S-curve rolltop desk; 65" wide, 36" deep, 50" high, $6,800.

S-curve rolltop desk with a patent date of 1884; 60" wide, 34" deep, 51" high, $5,750.

Student-size rolltop desk; 36 1/4" wide, 22" deep, 37" high. In Illinois, $495.

S-curve rolltop desk; 53 1/2" wide, 23 1/2" deep, 46" high. In Illinois, $1,750.

Rolltop desk; 60" wide, 34" deep, 42 1/2" high. In Illinois, $1,750.

Rolltop desk; 40" wide, 25" deep, 41" high. In Wisconsin, $1,750.

Cylinder desk with incised decorations; 32" wide, 22" deep, 49" high. In Wisconsin, $1,495.

Artificially grained (to imitate quarter-sawed oak) C-rolltop metal desk of the 1930s; 60" wide, 36" deep, 45" high. In Kentucky, $1,595.
←

S-curve rolltop desk with a plaque reading "Rowlett Desk Manufacturing Co., Richmond, Ind."; 54" wide, 20" deep, 48" high. In Illinois, $1,725.

S-rolltop desk; 42" wide, 30" deep, 46" high. In Iowa, $1,150.

→

Double-pedestal kneehole office desk that is paneled on the back so it can be positioned as a room divider; 53" wide, 25" deep, 30" high, $645.

Single-pedestal kneehole office desk; 36" wide, 27" deep, 31" high, $395.

LIBRARY

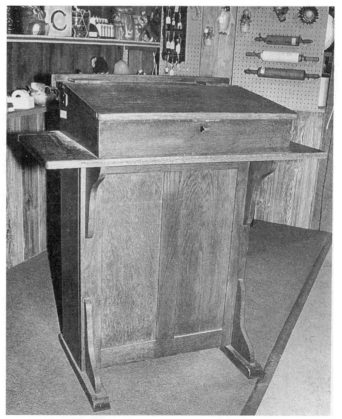

Desk with shelves on each side for book or magazine storage; 38" wide, 24" deep, 30" high, $395.

Schoolmaster's slant lift-top desk with storage space at front; 38" wide, 20" deep, 41" high. In Illinois, $495.

Swivel office chair made by Murphy, Owensberg, Kentucky; 33" high. In Michigan, $695 for the chair and desk combination.

Single pedestal desk made by Murphy, Owensberg, Kentucky; 42" wide, 32" deep, 33" high. In Michigan, $695 for the chair and desk combination.

Desk with three drawers and applied decorations on back rail; 28" wide, 17" deep, 36" high. In Illinois, $395.

→

Kneehole partner's desk with provisions on each side for a worker. Top lifts off the double pedestal base for easier transporting; 60" wide, 49" deep, 31" high. In Iowa, $975.

Quarter-sawed oak table desk with Queen Anne legs; 41" wide, 21" deep, 32" high. In Illinois, $545.

Cane seat and back swivel chair with bent parts made of hickory or elm; 20" arm to arm, $375.

Swivel pressed-back cane seat chair; 22" arm to arm, 42" high, $495.

Swivel office chair; 24" arm to arm, $245.

Swivel office chair; 24" arm to arm, $245.

Swivel cane seat chair; 22" arm to arm, 43" high, $375.

Swivel cane seat chair; 22" arm to arm, 41" high, $375.

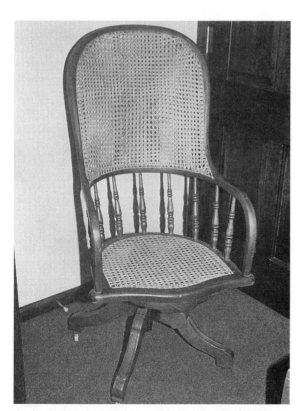

Elm swivel desk chair that tilts and revolves with cane seat; 24" arm to arm, 46 1/2" high. In Illinois, $450.

Swivel desk chair that tilts and revolves, made of oak, ash, maple, and elm for bending; 21" arm to arm, 45 1/2" high. In Iowa, $475.

Swivel office chair; 23" arm to arm, 38" high. In Iowa, $395.

Swivel desk chair; 23" arm to arm, 35" high. In Iowa, $295.

Elm swivel desk chair; 25" arm to arm, 47" high. In Wisconsin, $425.

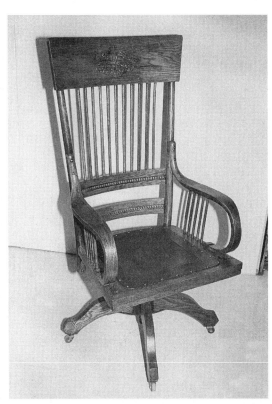

Pressed-back swivel office chair; 23" arm to arm, 45" high. In Illinois, $345.

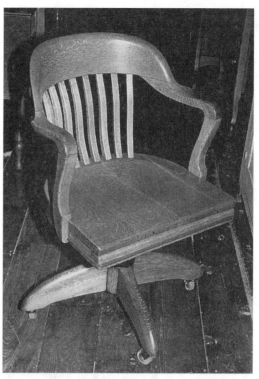

*Cane-seat single-pressed-back swivel chair; 24"
arm to arm, 46" high. In Iowa, $415.*

*Swivel office chair; 23" arm to arm, 34" high.
In Illinois, $225.*

Office armchair, $215.

*Office armchair with handhold in back rail,
$225.*

LIBRARY

Office armchair, $225.

Office armchair, $195.

Armchair with cane seat and back; 21" arm to arm, 36" high. $345.

Bookcase with adjustable shelves, currently used to store and display china and glass; 39" wide, 14" deep, 57" high, $745.

Double-section bookcase with rolled waterfall-type top and paw feet; 44" wide, 13" deep, 59" high, $945.

Book-case with plank sides, incised lines, and carved cornice. Original owner purchased this with his first month's pay as a school-teacher; 42" wide, 12" deep, 81" high, $1,250.

Bookcase with open and closed storage space; 27" wide, 12" deep, 53" high, $735.

Bookcase with applied decorations; 41" wide, 13" deep, 78" high, $1,250.

Bookcase with applied beading around glass door panels, circa 1920s; 39" wide, 15" deep, 62" high, $895.

Bookcase; 48" wide, 13" deep, 51" high, $895.

Folding bookshelf; 24" wide, 8" deep, 44" high. In Colorado, $255.

Bookcase; 38 1/2" wide, 13" deep, 53" high. In Iowa, $895.

Bookcase with paw feet; 40" wide, 13" deep, 59" high. In Illinois, $955.

Bookcase with latticework on top door panels and applied decorations; 39" wide, 12 1/2" deep, 72" high. In Iowa, $1,750.

Bookcase; 39" wide, 11 1/2" deep, 57 1/2" high. In Wisconsin, $865.

LIBRARY

Bookcase with three doors and four front paw feet; 55" wide, 14" deep, 60" high. In Wisconsin, $1,250.

Bookcase with three doors and paw feet; 55 1/4" wide, 14" deep, 67 1/2" high. In Indiana, $1,650.

Bookcase with three front legs and applied decorations on stiles; 40" wide, 18" deep, 57" high. In Michigan, $945.

Bookcase with applied decorations on back rail; 36" wide, 13" deep, 66" high. In Illinois, $855.

Bookcase; 40" wide, 14" deep, 76" high. In Illinois, $745.

Bookcase; 40" wide, 13" deep, 45" high. In Tennessee, $695.

Bookcase with leaded glass at the top of the flat glass doors and paw feet; 61" wide, 12" deep, 63" high. In Iowa, $1,450.

Bookcase with pressed carving; 43" wide, 12" deep, 48" high. In Wisconsin, $725.

Single-door bookcase; 31" wide, 14" deep, 61" high with 6" top rail. In Michigan, $545.

Bookcase with leaded glass at the top of the two flat glass doors and a Larkin label on the back; 42" wide, 14" deep, 58" high. In Iowa, $895.

Bookcase with two doors and applied decoration on back rail; 41" wide, 14" deep, 70" high. In Illinois, $1150.

Stack bookcase in five sections with doors that pull up and slide in; 34" wide, 12" deep, 47" high, $625.

Stack bookcase in five sections with doors that pull up and slide in; 34" wide, 13" deep, 43" high, $685.

Stack book-case with doors that pull up and slide in, originally finished in fumed oak, in six sections with leaded glass in the upper section and a label reading "Gunn Sectional Bookcase, pat., Dec. 5, 1899; June 1, 1901, Grand Rapids"; 34" wide, 12" deep, 66" high, $945.

Stack bookcase in six sections with doors that pull up and slide in, used as a china cabinet; 34" wide, 14" deep, 56" high, $795.

Stack bookcase in five sections with doors that pull up and slide in; 34" wide, 11" deep, 51" high, $625.

Combination stacking bookcase-desk, called "The Herkiner," made by F.E. Hale Mfg. Co., Herkiner, N.Y.; 34" wide, 14" deep, 59" high. In Michigan, $950.

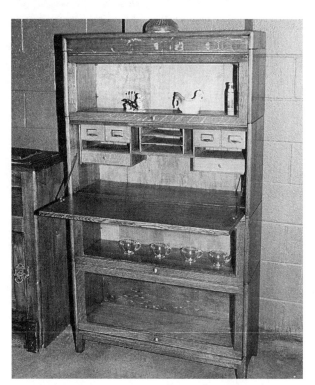

Combination bookcase-desk made in six sections; 34" wide, 12" deep, 60" high. In Illinois, $895.

Bookcase in five sections with three doors that pull up and slide in; 34" wide, 11" deep, 50" high. In Iowa, $755.

Bookcase in six sections with four leaded glass doors that pull up and slide in; 35 1/2" wide, 14" deep, 65" high. In Iowa, $995.

Bookcase in six sections with four glass doors that pull up and slide in; 34" wide, 11" deep, 59" high. In Iowa, $845.

Larkin sectional bookcase with instructions that include assembly techniques; 34" wide, 12" deep, 44" high. In Iowa, $795.

Viking sectional bookcase made by Skandia Furniture Co., Rockford, Ill., patented 1908; 34" wide, 13" deep, 57" high. In Wisconsin, $545.

Macey sectional bookcase with bottom drawer and claw feet; 34" wide, 11" deep, 69" high. In Iowa, $750.

Sectional bookcase; 34" wide, 11" deep, 61" high. In Wisconsin, $650. ←

Macey sectional bookcase; 34" wide, 12" deep, 49" high. In Indiana, $650.

Globe-Wernicke sectional bookcase made in Cincinnati, Ohio; 34" wide, 10" deep, 62" high. In Iowa, $695.

LIBRARY

Stack bookcase with fall-front desk and leaded glass top door; 35" wide, 12" deep, 62" high. In Alaska, $995.

←

Library table with twisted and spool-turned legs; 34" wide, 22" deep, 28" high, $475.

Oval library table with handleless drawer and pillar legs; 38" wide, 24" deep, 30" high, $495.

Library table with grooved legs; 32" wide, 23" deep, 30" high, $465.

Library table; 36" wide, 24" deep, 28" high. In Iowa, $575.

LIBRARY

Library table with curved apron, lyre-type legs and paw feet; 45" wide, 26" deep, 30" high, $695.

Library table with lyre-type legs; 42" wide, 26" deep, 29" high, $495.

LIBRARY

Library table with cabriole legs; 29" wide, 22" deep, 29" high, $495.

←

Piano bench converted into a coffee table; 39" wide, 19" deep, 21" high, $155.

→

Cut-down library table with two supporting pillars and ball feet; 36" wide, 24" deep, 19" high. In Michigan, $595.

Folding lady's desk; 32" wide, 17 1/2" deep, 26 1/2" high. In Illinois, $275.

Library table with pressed design on drawer and apron and base shelf; 36" wide, 23" deep, 29" high. In Iowa, $465.

Library table with one drawer at each end and scroll feet; 42" wide, 28" deep, 30" high. In Michigan, $495.

Library table with ball and stick construction on base shelf, beading on apron, and incised decorations; 36" wide, 24" deep, 31" high. In Wisconsin, $475.

Library table; 36" wide, 24" deep, 28" high. In Wisconsin, $465.

Library table; 48" wide, 29" deep, 30" high. In Iowa, $575.

Library table with one drawer and book shelves; 40" wide, 25" deep, 30" high. In Michigan, $425.

→

Library table with cabriole legs and base shelf; 36" wide, 24" deep, 29" high. In Michigan, $425.

→

Imperial Furniture Co., Grand Rapids, Michigan, quarter-sawed oak library table with applied tenons on legs and side stretchers, slatted sides, and triangular-shaped copper drawer pull; 50" wide, 32" deep, 30" high, $450.

←

Fourteen-drawer, stepback file cabinet; 33" wide, 25" deep at base, 17 deep at top, 62" high. In Iowa, $850.

File cabinet, originally property of the United States Army Air Forces; 20" wide, 25" deep, 53" high, $525.

File cabinet with 36 drawers, originally used in the University of Iowa library; 42" wide, 17" deep, 35" high, $900.

File cabinet with four drawers; 13" wide, 16" deep, 9" high, $185.

Four-drawer file cabinet; 14 1/2" wide, 24 1/2" deep, 52" high. In Iowa, $545.

Six-stack file cabinet; 13 1/4" wide, 15" deep, 29 1/2" high. In Iowa, $425.

Six-drawer file cabinet manufactured by Yawman & Erbe Mfg. Co., Rochester, New York; 11 1/4" wide, 15" deep, 14 1/2" high. In Iowa, $375.

Combination bookcase-file cabinet dated 1903, used either in a library or office; 41" wide, 17" deep, 60" high. In Wisconsin, $1,295.

Sixteen-drawer library card catalog file; 14 1/2" wide, 20" deep, 52" high. In Colorado, $525.

Close-up showing how each section of the card catalog file can be removed from its case.

Nine-drawer stack file cabinet manufactured by Yawman & Erbe Mfg. Co., Rochester, New York; 33" wide, 18" deep, 17 1/2" high. In Wisconsin, $285.

Four-drawer file cabinet with mission-style sides; 18" wide, 24" deep, 52" high. In Iowa, $545.

Six-drawer file cabinet; 33" wide, 24" deep, 34" high. In Indiana, $395.

Filing and storage cabinet; 32" wide, 24" deep, 63" high. In Michigan, $1,250.

Fifty-four-drawer file cabinet made by W.C. Heller & Co., Montpelier, Ohio; 26" wide, 12" deep, 43" high. In Wisconsin, $975.

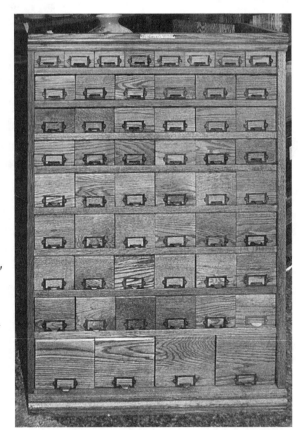

File cabinet with four drawers; 18" wide, 18" deep, 44" high. In Iowa, $645.

Four-drawer file cabinet; 15" wide, 24" deep, 51" high. In Iowa, $545.

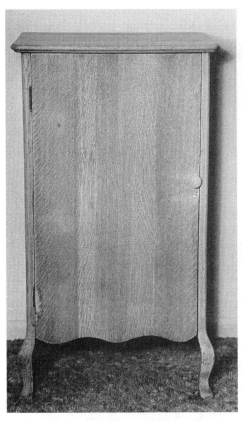

Music cabinet used to store sheet music, records, or player piano rolls; 18" wide, 16" deep, 34" high, $255.

←

Record cabinet for 150 records, made by Pooley Furniture Co., Philadelphia, Pa., patented December 27, 1910; 28" wide, 21" deep, 36" high. In Michigan, $425.

Music cabinet with five shelves inside and beveled mirror at top; 18" wide, 15" deep, 45" high. In Michigan, $375.

Music cabinet used to hold cylinders; 16 1/2" square, 33 1/2" high. In Illinois, $375.

LIBRARY

Music cabinet with five shelves inside; 18" square, 40" high. In Michigan, $465.

←

Music cabinet with mirror in back rail; 19" wide, 14" deep, 37" high, 9" rail. In Wisconsin, $345.

Columbia Regent desk phonograph; 46" wide, 29" deep, 31" high. On the top of the desk sits an Edison Amberola cylinder phonograph with 30 cylinders; 13" wide, 16" deep, 14" high. In Kentucky, Columbia Regent $850 and Edison, $465.

Victrola made by Victor Talking Machine Co., sold by Stack Piano Co., Chicago, Ill. $495.

Graphophone made by Columbia Phonograph Co., with latest patent date of March 30, 1897; 12" wide, 8" deep, 7" high, $795.

Coin-operated Regina music box with cylinders; 24" wide, 17" deep, 49" high. In Iowa, $5,250.

Symphoniom music box with 15" disks; 24" wide, 20 1/2" deep. In Colorado, $3,750. Parlor table; 29 1/2" square, 31 1/2" high, $425.

Edison phonograph with latest patent date of Nov. 17, 1903; 13" wide, 9" deep, 12" high, $795.

Graphophone, made by the Columbia Phonograph Co. of New York, patented March 20, 1897; used the standard cylinder and the 5" cylinder by removing the cylinder holder; 15" wide, 11 1/2" deep, 10" high. In Iowa, $2,195.

*Edison cylinder phono-
graph with metal horn, patented May 31, 1898; 16 1/2"
wide, 7 1/2" deep, 11" high.
In Iowa, $955.*

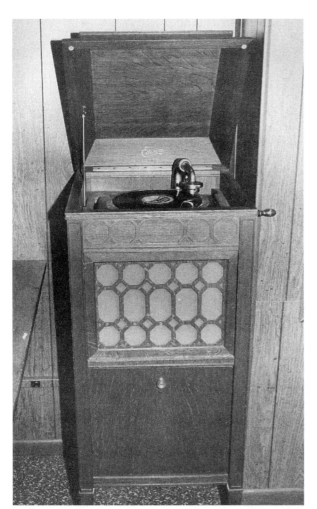

*Edison phonograph, sold at Kennedy Music Co.,
Dixon, Illinois, patented 1916; 19" wide, 20" deep,
45" high. In Illinois, $445.*

*Table model Victrola with label on horn reading
"flower horn;" 11 1/2" square base, 19" diameter
horn, 20" long. In Illinois, $995.*

Table model Columbian Graphophone with red morning glory horn; 13 1/2" square base, 19" diameter horn. In Colorado, $1,250.

Edison Gem Phonograph, patented October 3, 1905, Orange, New Jersey; 10" wide, 8" deep, 9" high with cover on. In Indiana, $695.

Edison Standard Phonograph with blue morning-glory horn, patented May 32, 1898, Orange, New Jersey; 12" wide, 9" deep, 12" high with cover on; horn 17" diameter. In Indiana, $845.

Epworth organ made by Williams Organ Co., Chicago, Ill.; 55" wide, 30" deep, 47" high, $1,250.

Windsor organ; 43 1/2" wide, 24" deep, 75" high. In Iowa, $2450.

Piano stool; 15" diameter, 21" high as pictured, $195.

Piano stool that adjusts in height; 14 1/2" diameter. In Illinois, $215.

Piano stool with claw and glass-ball feet; 12" diameter, 20" high. In Michigan, $195.

→

Piano stool with claw and glass ball feet; 14" diameter, 19" high. In Illinois, $155.

Piano or organ stool with metal claw and glassball feet; 14" diameter, 19" high in down position. In Illinois, $155.

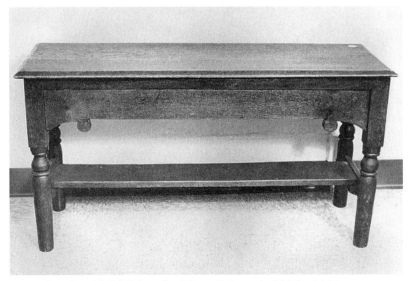

Piano bench with lift lid; 41" wide, 14" deep, 21" high, $165.

Chapter 8

The Bedroom

The bedroom was the center of life in the homes of the late 1800s. This was where babies were born and where the extremely sick spent the last days of their lives.

Furnishings often consisted of a three-piece matching bedroom set with a bed, dresser, and a washstand. A washstand commode provided space for a washbowl and pitcher. Other parts of the chamber set included a toothbrush holder and a covered soap dish. Because most homes lacked running water, family members or servants had to carry water to various rooms. If, in the wintertime, the used water was not discarded after bedtime use, it could turn to ice by morning. Central heating was unknown.

Bedroom pieces were sold individually or as a set. Applied or incised designs were commonly present on the head and footboard of a bed. Decorations that have a scooped out appearance are often called spoon carvings, but originally were called chip carvings.

Dressers with swing mirrors, or those called Chevals, provided cabinet space. Cheval dressers have a tall looking glass above two long low drawers. Another type of dresser was referred to as a Princess dresser. It had either two long drawers below a swing mirror or a combination of two small parallel drawers and one long drawer.

Chiffoniers were tall, narrow chests of drawers that provided another storage site in the bedchamber. Many had five levels of drawers. The top two were often smaller drawers side by side. Below would be four large drawers. Chiffoniers often featured a serpentine front that rippled in and out in snake-like fashion.

Projection tops refer to case pieces that have a drawer that hangs out over its lower section. An expensive version might include a side lock that has a hidden strip of wood that covers one stile. This swings open and unlocks all of the drawers when the key is turned.

When bedroom furniture was being made, manufacturers realized that a primping place was needed for the ladies. For this reason, dressing tables with mirrors were created. A matching stool or chair was included. For obvious reasons, this furniture was also known as a vanity.

Folding beds have dual functions. An 1897 mail order catalog shows a combination folding bed, wardrobe, and writing desk. Another unique bed, not a part of a bedroom set, was called a "Murphy" bed. Early 20th century catalogs described this type of hide-a-bed or fold-up unit as "a combination, mantel, or upright." In some Murphy types, a bed was available when it was in the pulled down position and was transformed into a bookcase or combination wardrobe/desk when it was closed.

Because closets were not present in most homes, chifforobes or wardrobes provided the necessary space to store clothes. The chifforobe had drawers on one side and closet space on the other. Wardrobes were usually designed with a shelf at the top. A hanging rod was provided for garments. The base was comprised of one or two drawers.

Because the wardrobes were usually large and bulky, they were difficult to transport – particularly to the upper level of the house where bedrooms were located. Manufacturers solved this problem when they constructed collapsible pieces that could be carried more easily. Breakdowns is another name for this style. Today, wardrobes often are not used as originally intended. They often serve as entertainment centers, providing space for TVs, stereos, and related articles.

The use of oak veneers is shown in a 1923-1924 Montgomery Ward catalog, in contrast to the solid oak used in previous years. As the supply of oak was dwindling, other woods and veneers began replacing oak as the dominant wood. Veneered bedroom sets in walnut with burled mahogany decorations copied various early furniture styles including Queen Anne, Adam, and Louis XVI. Painted furniture and metal examples also existed. About this time, oak's period of popularity was coming to an end.

Three-piece bedroom set with applied decorations and incised lines. Bed is 64" wide, 73" high headboard, 33" high footboard; dresser is 43" wide, 19" deep, 73" high; washstand is 32" wide, 15" deep, 37" high, $4,150.

←

Three-piece quarter-sawed bedroom set: bed 56" wide, headboard 48" high; washstand with towel bar top, 32" wide, 19" deep, 49 1/2" high; dresser with swing mirror, 44" wide, 22" deep, 66" high. In Wisconsin, $2,975 for the three-piece set.

Three-piece bedroom set with spoon carving: bed, 54 1/2" wide, headboard 69 1/2" high; dresser with swing mirror, 40 1/2" wide, 18 1/2" deep, 72" high; washstand, 30" wide, 16 1/4" deep, 29" high, 7" back rail. In Iowa, $3,250 for the three-piece set.

*Two-piece bedroom set: bed, 57" wide, headboard 72" high;
dresser with swing mirror, 41" wide, 18" deep, 78 1/2" high. In Wisconsin, $1,950 for the two-piece set.*

*Two-piece bedroom set: bed with applied decorations, 60" wide,
headboard 78" high; dresser with serpentine front, applied decorations, and swing mirror, 44" wide, 22"
deep, 80" high. In Wisconsin, $1,950 for the two-piece set.*

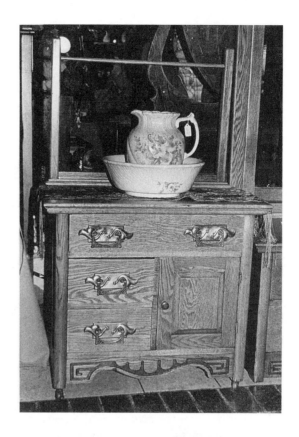

Three-piece bedroom set; bed, 58" wide, headboard 41" high; cheval dresser with hat cabinet and two small drawers, 45" wide, 20" deep, 72" high; washstand, 32" wide, 18" deep, 49" high. In Iowa, $3,750 for the three-piece set.

Two-piece bedroom set comprising a cheval dresser with hatbox and tall cheval mirror; 45" wide, 19" deep, 81" high; and a bed 59" wide, 27" high footboard, 68" high headboard. In Illinois, $1,450 for the set.

Commode washstand with metal towel bar on side; 32" wide, 18" deep, 29" to top, 13" back rail. In Indiana, part of a three-piece bedroom set with the dresser not pictured, $3,850 for the set.

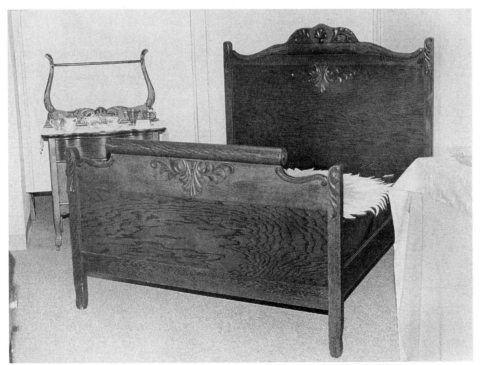

Bed and washstand commode with towel bar; bed 57" wide, 35" high footboard, 53" high headboard; commode 32" wide, 17" deep, 48" high. In Wisconsin, $1,250 for the set.

Ash commode washstand with applied decorations, mirror and attached towel bar; 33" wide, 18" deep, 72" high. In Wisconsin, $645.

Commode washstand with mirror and towel bar back and serpentine drawer; 36" wide, 18" deep, 72" high. In Illinois, $595.

Mixed woods (ash, chestnut, and oak) Eastlake marble-top washstand commode with burl veneer drawer panels, chip carving, and incised lines; 28" wide, 16" deep, 40" high, $725.

BEDROOM

Ash washstand commode with incised lines and pressed brass backplates and bail handles; 31" wide, 16" deep, 30" high, $425.

→

BEDROOM

The back of the ash washstand shows the factory marking.

→

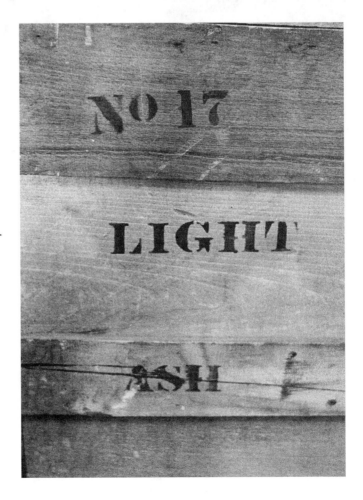

Washstand commode with incised lines and spoon carving; 32" wide, 19" deep, 36" high, $445.

→

BEDROOM

Washstand commode with incised lines; 30" wide, 17" deep, 30" high, $355.

Washstand commode with applied decorations, projection serpentine drawer, and towel bar back; 34" wide, 20" deep, 53" high, $395.

Washstand commode with projection serpentine drawer and towel bar back; 33" wide, 19" deep, 56" high, $395.

Washstand commode with towel bar removed but available; 33" wide, 17" deep, 26" high, $375.

Marble-top washstand commode with incised lines and designs; 32" wide, 18" deep, 28" high, $495.

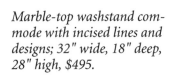

Washstand commode with towel bar back; 36" wide, 19" deep, 44" high, $445.

←

Lift-top "sick room" commode; 16" square, 16" high. In Ohio, $195.

Victorian-style washstand commode with white marble top; 30 1/2" wide, 16 1/4" deep, 28 1/2" high, 7" splashback. In Wisconsin, $465.

Marble-top washstand commode with incised lines; 32" wide, 17" deep, 34" high, $595.

Wash-stand com-mode with incised lines and spoon carving designs; 30" wide, 17" deep, 30" high, $395.

Washstand with replaced splashback and new brass pulls; 30 1/2" wide, 15 1/4" deep, 29 1/4" high; splashback 7 1/2". In Iowa, $355. Ash, elm, and maple chair; 40 1/2" high. In Iowa, $97.50.

Washstand commode with projection serpentine drawer and swing mirror; 32" wide, 18" deep, 52" high, $445.

BEDROOM

Sideboard. This is an example of a marriage candidate if a back were added; 45" wide, 22 1/2" deep, 38" high. In Iowa, $325.

Ash commode washstand; 35" wide, 21" deep, 34" high. In Michigan, $425.

BEDROOM

Washstand with roll front drawer and small swing mirror; 38" wide, 19 1/2" deep, 60" high. In Illinois, $545.

Washstand with serpentine projection top drawer; 32" wide, 17" deep, 30" high, 7 1/2 splashback. In Michigan, $425.

Washstand with quarter-sawed serpentine drawer and doors that are veneered; 33" wide, 20" deep, 19 1/2" high. In Illinois, $425.

Washstand with towel bar top; 36" wide, 19" deep, 53 1/2" high. In Ohio, $455.

Washstand with applied decorations and serpentine projection drawer; 38" wide, 20" deep, 28 1/2" high, 4 1/2" splash-back. In Illinois, $465.

BEDROOM

Washstand with towel bar top; 32 1/2" wide, 16 1/2" deep, 53 1/2" high. In Illinois, $425.

Washstand with towel bar top; 30 1/2" wide, 17 1/2" deep, 54" high. In Iowa, $425.

BEDROOM

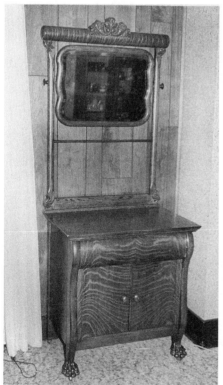

Washstand with combination towel bar-mirror top; and intricate paw feet; 30" wide, 21" deep, 68" high. In Indiana, $645.

←

Washstand commode with replaced towel bar and serpentine drawer front; 32" wide, 19" deep, 51" high. In Iowa, $395.

Washstand with combination towel bar-mirror top; and intricate paw feet; 30" wide, 21" deep, 68" high. In Indiana, $645.

Wash-stand with side-by-side towel bar and mirror top; 40" wide, 18" deep, 65" high. In Illinois, $545.

Oak and elm commode washstand; 32" wide, 18" deep, 30" high with 5" rail. In Michigan, $395.

Washstand with side-by-side towel bar and mirror top; 32" wide, 19" deep, 64" high. In Pennsylvania, $455.

BEDROOM

Hotel washstand with lift lid that exposes a white marble basin and drain board. Label on back reads, "The Windsor Combination Washstand, Pat. Jan. 14, 1890. The Windsor Folding Bed Co., Chicago." 31" wide, 27" deep, 58" high. In Kentucky, $1800.
→

The Windsor Combination Washstand showing the white marble basin and drain board.

BEDROOM

Washstand commode with towel bar and serpentine drawer front; 31" wide, 17" deep, 51" high. In Illinois, $395.

Ash bureau commode with walnut applied panels, knobs and escutcheons, circa 1870; 30" wide, 17" deep, 33" high with a 6" rail. In Michigan, $495.

Ash commode washstand with towel bar that is not original; 30" wide, 18" deep, 59" high. In Illinois, $415.

Commode washstand with towel bar and serpentine drawer front; 33" wide, 18" deep, 60" high. In Wisconsin, $415.

Elm and ash commode washstand with towel bar and serpentine drawer front; 34" wide, 19" deep, 53" high. In Iowa, $465.

Painted oak washstand (paint can hide defects); 30" wide, 15" deep, 29" high; splashback 5 1/2". In Virginia, $295.

Wash-stand; 21 1/2" wide, 15 1/2" deep, 29 1/2" high, 3 1/4" splash-back. In Iowa, $255.

A hatbox that has been removed from a cheval dresser. The back rail has been added; 16" wide, 15" deep, 22" to top, 3" back rail. In Indiana, $245.

BEDROOM

Nightstand with cabriole legs and serpentine front; 22" wide, 16" deep, 30" high. In Iowa, $265.

Combination desk-washstand made by Windsor Folding Bed, patented June 9, 1885; 31" wide, 27" deep at base, 66" high, $1,595.

Bed with applied decorations; 57" wide (lengthened to 84"), 57" high headboard, 37" high footboard, $565.

Ash three-quarter size bed with walnut trim on foot and headboards; 52" wide, 81" long, $425.

Bed with applied decorations; 59" wide, 79" long, 60" high headboard, $575.

Single bed with applied decorations; 40" wide, 76" long, $475.

BEDROOM

Bed with applied decorations; 56 1/2 " wide, headboard 65" high. In Iowa, $545.

Bed with roll tops on foot and headboard, and scroll feet; 55" wide, 41" high footboard, 47" high headboard. In Illinois, $275.

Single bed with applied decorations; 45" wide, 50" high headboard, 30" high footboard. In Illinois, $425.

Bed with applied decorations, 57" wide, 74" high. In Illinois, $545.

Bed with applied decorations and roll on footboard, 56 1/2" wide; headboard 46" high. In Illinois, $695.

Bed with applied decorations on head- and footboards; 57" wide, 39" high footboard, 79" high headboard. In Tennessee, $595.

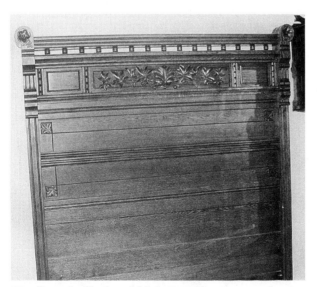

Headboard of bed; 76" high. In Indiana, part of a three-piece bedroom set, $4,150 for the set.

Bed with spoon carving; 58" wide, 33" high footboard, 75" high headboard. In Kentucky, $545.

Bed with applied decorations; 58" wide, 35" high footboard, 79" high headboard. In Wisconsin, part of a two-piece bedroom set with the dresser not pictured, $1,595 for the set.

Bed with applied decorations; 59" wide, 34" high footboard, 73" high headboard. In Iowa, $495.

Bed with applied decorations on head- and footboards; 58 1/2" wide, 78 1/4" long, 82" high at headboard. In Iowa, $550.

→

Murphy or mantel bed with mirror in top rail and applied decorations; 55" wide, 19" deep, 63" high, $1,650.

Combination folding bed (missing), bookcase, and writing desk; 55" wide, 27" deep, 77" high. In Kentucky, $1,650.

Murphy bed in open position.

Cheval dresser with applied drawer panels and incised decorations; 41" wide, 20" deep, 77" high. In Illinois, $745.

←

Cheval dresser with hat cabinet, incised lines, and decorations; 48" wide, 21" deep, 82" high, $795.

→

BEDROOM

Cheval mirror used for shaving and makeup; 20" wide, 9" deep, 25" high, $295.

Cheval dresser with hat cabinet and applied decorations; 42" wide, 21" deep, 76" high, $755.

Cheval dresser with hat cabinet and two small drawers; 42" wide, 18" deep, 81 1/2" high. In Illinois, $695.

Cheval dresser with hat cabinet and two small drawers; 42" wide, 20" deep, 78 1/2" high. In Iowa, $645.

Cheval dresser with hatbox and tall cheval mirror; 44" wide, 21" deep, 77" high. In Indiana, $695.

Eastlake cheval dresser with swing mirror, spoon carvings, incised lines and applied drawer and door panels; 41" wide, 19" deep, 77" high. In Illinois, $755.

BEDROOM

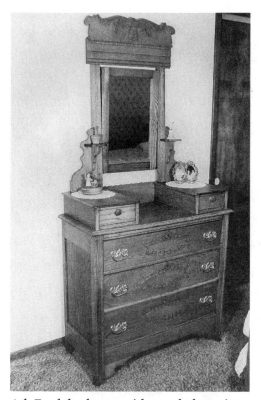

Ash Eastlake dresser with two decks, swing mirror, applied decorations and candle-stands; 37" wide, 17" deep, 76" high, $695.

Artificial-oak-grained dresser to resemble quarter-sawed oak; 44" wide, 23" deep, 76" high. $315.

Dresser with applied decorations, swing mirror, and serpentine drawers; 40" wide, 20" deep, 84" high, $595.

Dresser with swing mirror; 42" wide, 20" deep, 65" high, $495.

BEDROOM

Dresser with applied decorations and swing mirror; 44" wide, 22" deep, 76" high, $545.

Dresser with applied decorations, serpentine drawers, and swing mirror, 42" wide, 20" deep, 77" high, $525.

Dresser with applied decorations, swing mirror, and serpentine drawers; 41" wide, 19" deep, 72" high, $525.

Dresser with applied decorations, triple mirror, and serpentine drawers; 42" wide, 22" deep, 75" high, $795.

Dresser with applied decorations and swing mirror; 40" wide, 19" deep, 70" high, $525.

Ash dresser with applied decorations and wishbone mirror; 41" wide, 19" deep, 77" high, $845.

Princess dresser with swell projection center drawer and swing mirror; 42" wide, 20" deep, 65" high, $525.

Princess dresser with applied decorations, serpentine drawers, and swing mirror; 42" wide, 22" deep, 68" high, $495.

BEDROOM

Princess dresser with applied decorations, serpentine drawers and swing mirror; 40" wide, 21" deep, 71" high. $515.

Princess dresser with applied decorations and swing mirror; 41" wide, 21" deep, 73" high, $495.

Princess dresser with applied decorations, serpentine drawers, and swing mirror; 34" wide, 19" deep, 70" high, $525.

Elm dresser with applied decorations at top of frame; 42" wide, 20" deep, 79" high. In Alaska, $695.

Elm dresser with swing mirror; 42" wide, 21" deep, 74" high. In Illinois, $550.

Factory stamp found on the back of elm dresser.

BEDROOM

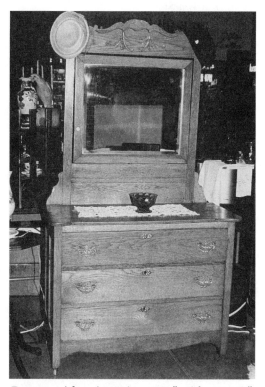

Dresser with swing mirror; 42" wide, 18 1/2" deep, 73" high. In Illinois, $545.

Dresser with serpentine front and swing mirror; 38" wide, 19 1/2" deep, 63" high. In Illinois, $625.

Hotel dresser with applied decorations, swing mirror, and serpentine side drawers; 46" wide, 23" deep, 71 1/2" high. In Colorado, $595.

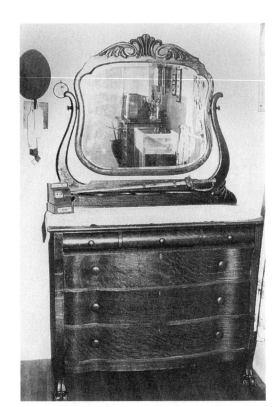

Dresser with swing mirror, three roll-front top drawers, three serpentine lower drawers, and paw feet; 44 1/2" wide, 22" deep, 74 1/4" high. In Iowa, $625.

Dresser with swing mirror; 38" wide, 18" deep, 68" high. In Iowa, $525.

Dresser with oval swing mirror and applied decorations; 34" wide, 21" deep, 75 1/2" high. In Iowa, $555.

Dresser with swing mirror and pressed design at crest; 41 1/2" wide, 19" deep, 69" high. In Michigan, $575.

Dresser with swing mirror, swell front, and applied leaf garlands on mirror frame; 45" wide, 21" deep, 76 1/4" high. In Illinois, $645.

BEDROOM

Dresser with swing mirror and applied decorations on mirror frame; 42" wide, 20" deep, 68 1/2" high. In Iowa, $595.

Princess dresser with swell front; 44" wide, 23" deep, 73" high. In Illinois, $595.

Dresser with serpentine top drawers and applied decorations on mirror frame; 45" wide, 22" deep, 78" high. In Michigan, $755.

Dresser with serpentine front, swing mirror and applied decorations; 40" wide, 21" deep, 76" high. In Illinois, $695.

Princess dresser with swing mirror and serpentine drawers; 40" wide, 21" deep, 73" high. In Iowa, $545.

Dresser with swing mirror, applied decorations and serpentine top drawers; 36" wide, 20" deep, 63" high. In Wisconsin, $525.

BEDROOM

Princess dresser with swing mirror, serpentine front and applied decorations on mirror and frame; 38" wide, 19" deep, 71" high. In Illinois, $565.

Dresser with three mirrors, two of which are adjustable for viewing; 42" wide, 19" deep, 64" high. In Michigan, $525.

BEDROOM

Dresser with serpentine front and applied decorations and grotesques on mirror frame; 38" wide, 20" deep, 70" high. In Illinois, $595.

Ash dresser with wishbone mirror, 5" high decks (handkerchief boxes), applied walnut circular molding on drawers and walnut pulls and escutcheons, circa 1870; 39" wide, 18" deep, 71" high. In Michigan, $825.

Dresser with swing mirror and applied decorations;42" wide, 19"deep, 77" high. In Wisconsin, $550.

Dresser with swing mirror and applied decorations; 43" wide, 19" deep, 74" high. In Illinois, $575.

Ash Victorian dresser with two decks or "hankie" boxes, applied carving on drawers and mirror frame, and candle or lamp shelves on mirror frame; 41" wide, 21" deep, 72" high. In Wisconsin, $895.

Dresser with swing mirror and applied decorations; 42" wide, 22" deep, 74" high. In Iowa, $595.

Ash Eastlake dresser with two decks or " hankie " boxes, incised designs, burl walnut panels on drawers, swing mirror, and candle or lamp shelves on mirror frame. Made in Lansing, Michigan; 39" wide, 18" deep, 80" high. In Michigan, $895.

Victorian ash dresser with walnut trim and fruit carved handles; 42" wide, 17" deep, 43" high. In Tennessee, $575.

BEDROOM

Ash dresser with 5" high decks (handkerchief boxes); 38" wide, 19" deep, 46" high. In Illinois, $495.

Chest of drawers with scribe lines and applied decorations on drawers; 41" wide, 18" deep, 42" high. In Iowa, $465.

Victorian dresser with applied decorations and projection top drawer; 40" wide, 19" deep, 42" high. In Wisconsin, $555.

Ash dresser, with walnut veneer panels on the drawers and a marble insert, is an example of Victorian manufacture; 37" wide, 17" deep, 39" high. In Illinois, $545.

Dresser with serpentine front and applied decorations on mirror and frame; 46" wide, 22" deep, 71" high. In Illinois, $625.

Quarter-sawed oak chiffonier with serpentine drawer fronts; 34" wide, 19" deep, 48" high, $595.

Chiffonier with serpentine drawers and door, hat cabinet, and cabriole legs; 34" wide, 18" deep, 48" high, $595.

Chiffonier with pilasters separating swell top drawers and door and paw feet; 42" wide, 22" deep, 47" high, $545.

Chiffonier with serpentine drawers; 30" wide, 19" deep, 40" high, $595.

Chiffonier with swell drawer fronts; 35" wide, 18" deep, 50" high, $595.

Chiffonier with incised lines; 33" wide, 18" deep, 41" high, $595.

Chiffonier with swell front and applied decorations on back rail; 33" wide, 19" deep, 59" high, $595.

Chiffonier with hatbox and incised lines; 36" wide, 19" deep, 55" high, $595.

Chiffonier with projection serpentine top drawers; 34" wide, 18" deep, 55" high, $515.

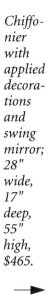

Chiffonier with applied decorations and swing mirror; 28" wide, 17" deep, 55" high, $465.

Chiffonier with projection top drawers and swing mirror; 33" wide, 19" deep, 71" high, $525.

Chiffonier with applied decorations and swing mirror; 33" wide, 18" deep, 72" high, $595.

BEDROOM

Chiffonier with scroll stiles and swing mirror supports, a style often called "colonial" in the 1920s catalogs; 36" wide, 20" deep, 69" high, $595.

←

Chiffonier with applied decorations and swing mirror; 34" wide, 19" deep, 70" high, $595.

Artificially grained oak chiffonier; 34" wide, 18" deep, 48" high. In Alaska, $475.

Chiffonier with quarter-sawed oak serpentine front; 33" wide, 19" deep, 48 1/2" high. In Illinois, $645.

BEDROOM

Chiffonier with swell sides, six lower serpentine drawers, and applied decorations; 34" wide, 20" deep, 50" high. In Michigan, $645.

Chiffonier with attached swing mirror and applied decorations; 34" wide, 18 1/2" deep, 63" high. In Illinois, $625.

Chiffonier with attached swing mirror and swell front; 30" wide, 19" deep, 70" high. In Illinois, $655.

Quarter-sawed oak chiffonier with attached swing mirror; 32" wide, 18" deep, 73 1/2" high. In Iowa, $595.

BEDROOM

BEDROOM

Ash hotel chiffonier with attached swing mirror, 30" wide, 17" deep, 63 1/2" high. In Colorado, $595.

Quarter-sawed oak chiffonier with attached swing mirror and scroll feet; 34" wide, 20" deep, 69" high. In Virginia, $595.

Chiffonier with serpentine front; 30" wide, 18" deep, 45" high. In Illinois, $525.

Chiffonier with serpentine front and applied decorations on mirror frame and support; 34" wide, 19" deep, 70" high. In Iowa, $725.

Chiffonier with swing mirror and bombe (swelling out) front and sides; 36" wide, 19" deep, 74" high. In Illinois, $795.

Chiffonier with three swell-front, parallel-top drawers and swing mirror; 42" wide, 21" deep, 70" high. In Alaska, $950.

Chiffonier with applied decorations on back rail and hat box; 33" wide, 19" deep, 45" high, 8" rail. In Iowa, $575.

Chiffonier with swing mirror and projection top drawer; 33" wide, 21" deep, 72" high. In Iowa, $695.

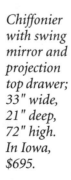

BEDROOM

Chiffonier with applied decorations on drawers and vertical beading on stiles; 33" wide, 20" deep, 50" high. In Indiana, $625.

Chiffo-nier with swing mirror and ser-pentine front; 33" wide, 18" deep, 72" high. In Ohio, $645.

→

Chiffonier with swing mirror; 28" wide, 19" deep, 71" high. In Wisconsin, $545.

→

Larkin chiffonier with serpentine top drawers and original label on the back; 34" wide, 19" deep, 51" high, 5" rail. In Iowa, $515.

L. and J.G. Stickley quarter-sawed oak highboy dresser with pegged construction and hand-hammered copper drawer pulls; 40" wide, 21" deep, 47" high; $1,795; with attached swing mirror, $2,695.

Chiffonier and fall-front desk combination with applied and incised decorations; 32" wide, 18" deep, 60" high. In Minnesota, $1,095.

Chifforobe with swing mirror, slide-out garment bar behind the closed door, and a fall-front desk surface; 43" wide, 19" deep, 68" high, $565.

Chifforobe with artificial grain to resemble quarter-sawed oak; 44 1/2" wide, 21 1/2" deep, 70 1/2" high. In Virginia, $395.

Chifforobe; 43 1/2" wide, 19 1/4" deep, 67" high. In Illinois, $425.

Ash wardrobe with incised lines and original wooden door panels replaced with glass; 40" wide, 16" deep, 78" high, $995.

Wardrobe with applied decorations and original wooden door panels replaced with glass; 48" wide, 18" deep, 96" high, $1,500.

Wardrobe converted into china cabinet by replacing wooden panels with glass and adding shelves; 42" wide, 12" deep, 68" high, $995.

←

BEDROOM

Wardrobe with beveled mirror, applied decorations, and pillars on stiles; 55" wide, 20" deep, 88" high, $1,450.

←

Wardrobe that breaks down for easier transportation; 43" wide, 17" deep, 83" high, $1,125.

Wardrobe with incised carving; 39" wide, 16" deep, 80" high, $945.

Wardrobe with incised carving and applied decorations; 44" wide, 16" deep, 82" high, $1,050.

Ash wardrobe; 44" wide, 17" deep, 84" high, $950.

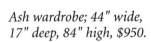

Artificially grained collapsible or breakdown wardrobe with two drawers at base; 48" wide, 17" deep, 86" high. In Illinois, $995.

Collapsible or breakdown wardrobe; 51" wide, 17" deep, 85" high. In Iowa, $1,500.

Wardrobe; 36" wide, 14" deep, 73" high. In Illinois, $995.

Wardrobe with applied decorations and molded door panels; 44" wide, 17" deep, 80" high, $945.

←

Wardrobe manufactured by the Marshall Furniture Co. of Henderson, Kentucky, makers of oak wardrobes and cabinets. Two bevel-glass mirrors, pilasters at sides and center, and intricately carved applied decorations, including grotesques (fish-like) flanking crest; 54 1/2" wide, 20" deep, 102" high. In Wisconsin, $3,150.

→

BEDROOM

Wardrobe; 39 1/2" wide, 16" deep, 83" high. In Iowa, $1,250.

Breakdown wardrobe with ornate cornice and two drawers at base; 48" wide, 17" deep, 94" high. In Illinois, $1,575.

Collapsible or breakdown wardrobe with applied decorations and two drawers at base; 44" wide, 16" deep, 80" high. In Iowa, $1,250.

Single-door wardrobe with one drawer; 34" wide, 17" deep, 78" high. In Illinois, $875.

Collapsible or breakdown wardrobe with two drawers and applied decoration at top; 51" wide, 19" deep, 82" high. In Illinois, $1,595.

BEDROOM

Dressing table with applied decorations, small swell drawers, cabriole legs, and swing mirror; 40" wide, 22" deep, 66" high, $995.

Dressing table with attached swing mirror and swell drawer front; 34 1/2" wide, 19" deep, 60" high. Chair 27" high. In Illinois, $645 for the two-piece set.

Dressing table; 36" wide, 17 1/2" deep, 57" high. In Illinois, $645.

Vanity and chair from the 1920s; vanity 40" wide, 20" deep, 57" high; chair 30" high. In Illinois, $525.

←

Dressing table or vanity with serpentine drawer and cabriole legs; 32" wide, 19" deep, 61" high. In Illinois, $595.

→

Dresser stand; 9" wide, 7" deep, 18 1/2" high. In Iowa, $295.

BEDROOM

Shaving stand with attached swing mirror and drop-front cabinet; 18" wide, 16" deep, 66" high. In Iowa, $675.

Mirror that was once a part of a cheval dresser; 22" wide, 52" high. In Wisconsin, $165.

Cheval mirror; 28" wide, 79" high. In Tennessee, $545.

One-drawer low chest that was probably the base of a cheval dresser; 48" wide, 22" deep, 17" high. In Michigan, $495.

Blanket chest with carved decoration on front and large copper-hinges; 35" wide, 18" deep, 18" high. In Michigan, $525.

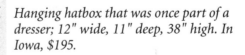

Hanging hatbox that was once part of a dresser; 12" wide, 11" deep, 38" high. In Iowa, $195.

Chapter 9

Chairs and Benches

In what part of the house do you usually find chairs? Because they fit into almost any location, chairs and benches are grouped in a chapter of their own. Diners, pressed-backs, T-backs, bentwoods, and cane chairs comprise the variety of chair styles that were available at the turn of the century.

The late 1800s and early 1900s catalogs give the name "diner" to those dining room chairs that were probably not made of oak. Included in this diner style are T-backs, the name given to chairs with backs that resemble a capital "T." Also available were the bent wood chairs created by Michael Thonet in Vienna, Austria around 1840. Soon this style was successfully mass-produced. Designer Thonet felt the style was strong, functional and aesthetically pleasing.

Cane chairs were abundant, but it was primarily the oak styles that were caned with pre-woven sheets of cane. The sheets were secured in an incised groove that circled the seat. When this was completed, measured strips of spleen were fitted into the glue covered router lines. Hand-caned examples also existed.

Heavily carved or embossed chairs were illustrated in the turn of the century catalogs. Today we call these chairs "pressed-backs." The design resulted when a metal die or mold stamped a shallow pattern, which resembled hand carving, into the backs. Heat, extreme pressure, and the quality of the die helped to achieve the carved appearance. Chiseling, used to supplement the look, resulted in a more deeply embossed effect. Double, triple, and quadruple designs were available. While examples with only the embossed top rail can be readily found, multi-pressed styles appear with less regularity.

A collection of early 20th century catalogs was perused to examine the time period of pressed-backs. During the fifty year span from the 1890s to the 1940s, the largest selection of pressed-backs was available in the 1890s catalogs. 1910 featured very few pressed-backs, and five years later, the catalogs were devoid of any examples.

While pressed-back designs of fish or grotesques are rare, flowers, garlands, and scrolls are common. Less commonly seen are such designs as a man blowing (now called "Man of the North Wind"), serpents, birds, and what appears to be mermaids, on chair backs. One pressed back has a Mother Goose design. Such rare designs are more costly.

Pressed-back designs have also shown patriotic motifs. A wooden seat chair with an impressed eagle and V on the back, dating to the 1940s, is pictured in this chapter. This blue applied V signifies the Victory symbol that Great Britain's World War II Prime Minister Winston Churchill presented to crowds when he raised two wide spread fingers.

Purchasing matched sets of pressed-back chairs in-groups of fours or sixes can be extremely costly. To cut costs, some collectors purchase individual, non-matching, chairs similar in design to make up a set.

Today, purchasers are buying the less expensive T-backs. These diners, with their square seats, were described in catalogs as "box seated" chairs not T-backs. The name T-back developed because of the singular perpendicular slat that was crossed at the top by a straight horizontal slat, resembling a capital "T".

By the 1920s, a dinette or breakfast-type chair was becoming popular. Some were brightly colored with black stencil designs, while others were stained or painted. A similarly decorated table formed a breakfast set with four accompanying chairs. These sets maintained their popularity through the 1940s.

In the late 1800s and early 1900s, rocking chairs proved to be relaxing, which resulted in many styles available. Those with more generous proportions accommodated the larger men. With their wide arms and spacious seats they were a comfortable place to sit, especially when the back curved to conform to the body's contours.

However, not everyone appreciated rocking chairs. The chair's occupant often feared that the rocker would tip over backwards. This fear has been substantiated by newspaper accounts from past years telling of individuals who were injured when they rocked off a porch. Perhaps, in order to overcome these problems, different companies acquired patents for platform rockers that glided back and forth on frames. They proved acceptable to sitters who disliked the conventional rocker, giving the user a feeling of security. These rockers were used extensively between 1890 and 1915. Originally they were known as "patent rockers."

Splat-back or T-back chair with leather seat, set of 6. $90 each.

Splat-back or T-back chair with upholstered seat; 37" high. In Iowa, $275 for a set of four.

Splat-back or T-back chair, set of 6. $135 each.

Splat-back or T-back upholstered-seat chair, set of 6. $125 each.

Splat-back or T-back upholstered-seat chair, set of 6. $125 each.

Bentwood cane seat armchair; 22" arm to arm, 35" high, set of 2. $185.

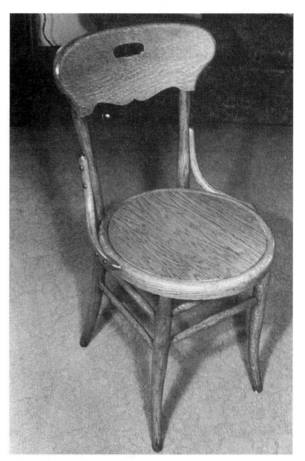

Side chair with handgrip. $145.

Bentwood ice cream chair; 33" high. In Illinois, $135.

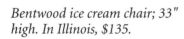

Bentwood barbershop chair; 38" high. In Illinois, $165.

Bentwood barbershop armchair; 23 1/2" arm to arm, 41" high. In Illinois, $185.

Slat back chair, 36" high. In Illinois, set of 6, $550.

Spindle-back cane seat chair, set of 4. $185 each.

Spindle-back cane seat chair, set of 6. $165 each.

Heywood-Wakefield cane seat chair, set of 4. $445.

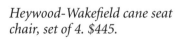

CHAIRS & BENCHES

Oak tilt-back cane chair with coil springs; hickory is used on the bent part where strength is essential; 21 1/2" arm to arm, 35" high. In Iowa, $395.

Cane seat side chair with demi arms has a Victorian influence; 34" high. In Wisconsin, $300 each in a set of four.

Cane seat side chair with concave front rung and finger hold on top rail; Victorian influence; 33" high. In Illinois, $165 each in a set of four.

←

Cane seat pressed-back chair with stick and ball design above back rail and below seat at front; 40" high. In Illinois. $215.

Cane seat chair with veneer back and heart-shaped fingerhold; 37" high. In Illinois, $135 each in a set of four.

Cane-seat chair; 19" arm to arm, 45" high. In Wisconsin, $210.

Woven cane-seat chair; 43" high. In Illinois, $155.

Pressed-back chair with solid seat, set of 6. $275 each.

Double-pressed-back cane-seat chair with fish design on back, set of 6. $260 each.

Close-up view of winged creature and prey on back of pressed-back chair.

←

Close-up of fish design on chair back. Elaborate patterns such as this one are unusual and add to a chair's price.

→

Double-pressed-back cane-seat armchair with fish design on back, set of 6. $280 each.

Pressed-back chair, set of 4. $165 each.

Double-pressed-back cane-seat chair, set of 6. $195 each.

Pressed-back chair, set of 6. $165 each.

Pressed-back solid-seat chair with Man of the North Wind design, set of 6. $275 each.

Close-up of Man of the North Wind.

Triple-pressed-back cane-seat chair, set of 6. $245 each.

Pressed-back cane-seat chair, set of 6. $195 each.

Pressed-back solid-seat chair with impressed designs on the front corners of the chair seat. $195.

Pressed-back solid-seat chair, set of 4. $155 each.

Pressed-back solid-seat chair, set of 4. $165 each.

Pressed-back cane-seat chair, set of 4. $185 each.

Pressed-back chair with cane seat, set of 4.
$695.

Pressed-back solid-seat chair with turnings that
resemble stacks of coins, set of 6. $195 each.

Pressed-back cane-seat chair with serpent-like
medallion on back, set of 4. $225 each.

Close up of serpent-like medallion on chair back.

Pressed-back cane-seat chair. $225.

Pressed-back chair with unusual pressed design on the seat around the cane, set of 2. $350 each.

Double-pressed-back cane-seat chair. $290.

Double-pressed-back chair. $195.

CHAIRS & BENCHES

Triple-pressed-back chair, set of 2. $295 each.

Triple-pressed-back cane-seat chair. $260.

Pressed-back cane-seat chair, set of 4. $165 each.

Pressed-back cane-seat chair, set of 6. $165 each.

Pressed-back cane-seat chair, set of 4. $165 each.

Cane seat pressed-back chair, 39" high. In Iowa, $810 for a set of six.

Oak pressed-back chair with some hand carving has a pressed cane seat and French front legs; 38" high. In Wisconsin, $145.

Elm pressed-back chair; 41" high. In Wisconsin, one of a set of four, $225 each.

Cane seat pressed-back chair; 40" high. In Colorado, $165.

Cane seat chair with pressed-back floral design; 41" high. In Ohio, $185.

Cane seat pressed-back chair, 39" high. In Michigan, $155.

Cane seat pressed-back chair; 41" high. In Illinois, $165.

Cane seat pressed-back chair; 35 1/2" high. In Illinois, $165.

Cane seat pressed-back chair with arrow back slats; 44" high. In Iowa, $825 for a set of four.

Cane seat double-pressed back chair, 41" high. In Michigan, $645 for a set of four.

Cane seat pressed-back chair, 41" high. In Iowa, $625 for a set of four.

Cane-seat pressed-back chair; 41" high. In Wisconsin. $375 for a set of two.

←

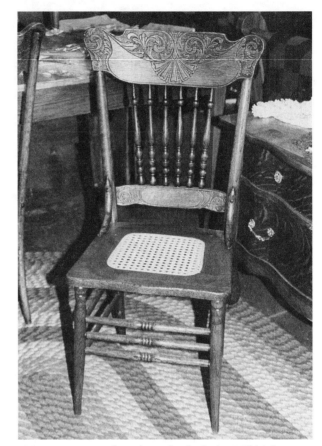

Cane-seat pressed-and-cut-back chair; 38" high. In Iowa, $475 for a set of three.

Cane-seat Man-of-the-Wind double-pressed-back chair; 42" high. In Illinois, $1,150 for a set of four.

Close-up of Man-of-the-Wind pressed back.

Cane-seat chair with veneered and pressed back; 39" high. In Tennessee, $595 for a set of four.

Wooden seat chair with impressed eagle and V on the back. Part of a set of four chairs and an extension table from the 1940s; 35" chair height; table 48" wide, 33" deep, 30" high. In Wisconsin, $495 for the five-piece set. ⟶

Cane-seat single-pressed-back chair; 39" high. In Wisconsin, $1,300 for a set of six.

Cane-seat single-pressed-back chair; 40" high. In Wisconsin, $525 for a set of four.

Cane-seat double-pressed-back chair; 42" high. In Iowa, $2,000 for a set of ten.

CHAIRS & BENCHES

A group of pressed designs are pictured here in order to illustrate the variety of patterns available.

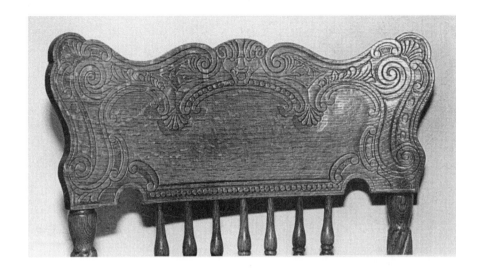

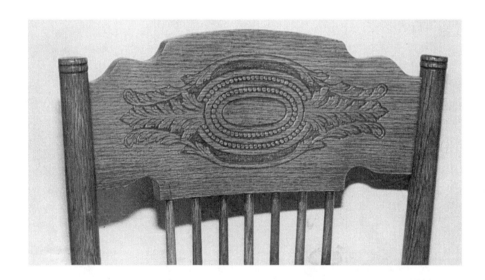

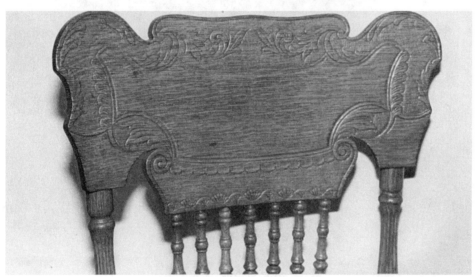

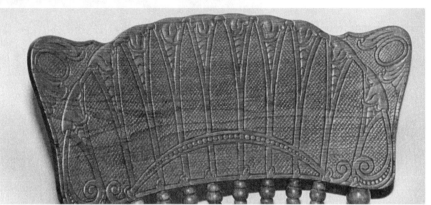

CHAIRS & BENCHES

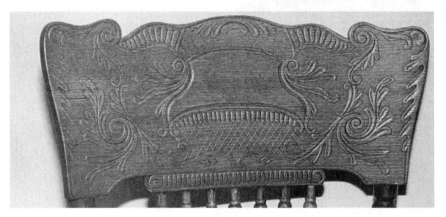

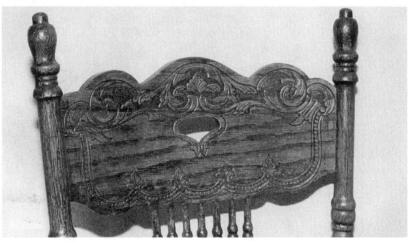

Rocker with upholstered seat and back; 26" arm to arm, 41" high. $245.

Shaker ladder-back rocker with woven seat; 22" arm to arm, 42" high. $515.

Pressed-back rocker with cane seat; 25" arm to arm, 36" high. $325.

Armchair rocker; 25" arm to arm, 40" high. $255.

CHAIRS & BENCHES

Cane seat ash rocker with sheaf of wheat impressed in top rail; 26" arm to arm, 43 1/2" high. In Iowa, $415.

Rocker with veneered back and rolled veneer seat; 26" arm to arm, 35" high. In Michigan, $445.

Rocker with pressed and carved lions' heads on back supports; 27" arm to arm. 36 1/2" high. In Wisconsin, $365.

Close-up of lion's head on upright post.

Upholstered rocker with tufted back and carved animal heads on arms; 27" arm to arm, 40" high. In Colorado, $545.

Close-up of animal head on rocker's arm.

Rocker with upholstered circle seat and finger hold in back rail; 22" arm to arm, 36" high. In Illinois, $415.

Cane seat rocker with pressed top rail and spindle back; 26" arm to arm, 41" high. In Iowa. $295.

Rocker with wicker curlicue scrolls and upholstered seat; 24" arm to arm, 46" high. In Michigan, $345.

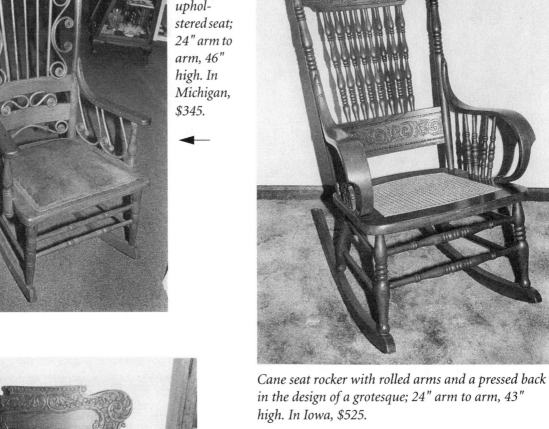

Cane seat rocker with rolled arms and a pressed back in the design of a grotesque; 24" arm to arm, 43" high. In Iowa, $525.

Cane seat rocker with pressed-back rail; 25" arm to arm, 43" high. In Iowa, $395.

Close-up of grotesque on back rail of rocker.

Cane seat rocker with rolled arms and a rare, fish-like, pressed-carved design on back rail; 22" arm to arm, 41 1/2" high. In Iowa, $645.

Rocker with grotesque in pressed back; 23 1/2" arm to arm, 37" high. In Wisconsin, $425.

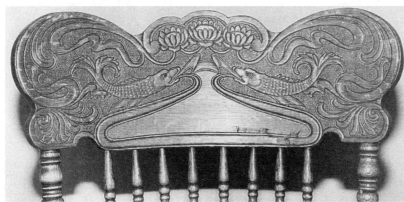

Close-up of the intricate pressed-carved design on back rail. ←

Close-up of grotesque on back rail of rocker. →

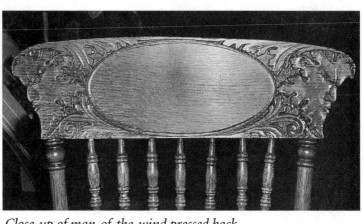

Close-up of man-of-the-wind pressed back.

Rocker with man-of-the-wind pressed back; 24" arm to arm, 40" high. In Illinois, $395.

Rocker with upholstered seat and grotesque carved on back panel; 25 1/2" arm to arm, 32" high. In Illinois, $525.

Bentwood (these parts were often made of ash, elm, or hickory) pressed cane-back platform rocker with upholstered seat; 21" arm to arm, 32" high. In Illinois, $425.

Rocker with upholstered seat; 24" arm to arm, 34" high. In Iowa. $345.

Rocker with applied decorations on veneered back; 23" arm to arm, 37" high. In Iowa, $295.

Rocker with spindles and upholstered seat; 23" arm to arm, 34" high. In Michigan. $365.

Veneered back rocker with applied decorations; 23" arm to arm, 36" high. In Illinois, $355.

CHAIRS & BENCHES

Cane-seat rocker with spindle back; 19" arm to arm, 42" high. In Iowa, $225.

Wooden seat single-pressed-back rocker; 28" arm to arm, 39" high. In Iowa, $315.

Veneered seat triple-pressed-back rocker; 25" arm to arm, 44" high. In Illinois, $310.

Cane-seat triple-pressed-back rocker; 24" arm to arm, 43" high. In Iowa, $495.

←

Rocker with wooden design surrounded by leather on back rail; 25" arm to arm, 39" high. In Wisconsin, $345.

Rocker with rolled veneer seat and back and finger hold; 23" arm to arm, 32" high. In Kentucky, $265.

Quadruple-pressed-back rocker with cane seat; 38" high. $185.

←

Pressed-back rocker with Man of the North Wind design; 39" high. $295.

Spindle-back rocker with splint seat; 39" high. $255.

→

Rocker with leather seat and spindled back; 42" high. $255.

Sewing rocker with cane seat and spindled back; 35" high. $235.

Cane seat lady's rocker; 39" high. In Illinois, $245.

Lady's pressed-back rocker; 38" high. In Illinois, $215.

Rocker with spindle back, brass straps on top rail and upholstered seat, 44" high. In Iowa, $235.

Cane-seat double-pressed-back rocker; 40" high. In Wisconsin, $255.

*Pressed- and carved-back
rocker with upholstered
seat; 37" high. In Iowa,
$255.*

*Cane-seat rocker with quarter-sawed back;
39" high. In Wisconsin, $245.*

Rocker with finger hold; 32" high. In Illinois, $215.

Rocker with demi-arms, needlepoint seat, and brass decorations on top slat; 43" high. In Tennessee, $245.

Cane-seat quadruple-pressed-back rocker; 38" high. In Iowa, $315.

Close-up of quadruple-pressed-back rocker.

Parlor armchair with floral crest on oval back, splayed legs, and H stretchers; 28" arm to arm, 39" high. $265.

Quarter-sawed and plain-sawed oak Roman chair with medallions, head carvings, and paw feet; 25" arm to arm, 38" high. $425.

Round-seat chair with cabriole legs and bent-wood hoop stretcher that pierces front legs; 22" arm to arm, 30" high. $265.

Armchair with black leather seat and back; 25" arm to arm, 41" high. In Iowa, $495.

CHAIRS & BENCHES

Armchair with applied decoration on top rail; 24" arm to arm. 45" high. In Iowa, $595.

Armchair with intricately carved head; 22 1/4" arm to arm. 41 1/2" high. In Illinois, $365.

Armchair with bentwood arms; 22" arm to arm, 43 1/2" high. In Illinois, $225.

Close-up of intricately carved chair back, called grotesque; 13 1/4" wide, 12" high.

Armchair with provision for pressed cane seat or seat of your choice; 23 1/2" arm to arm, 39" high. In Iowa, $275 each in a set of six.

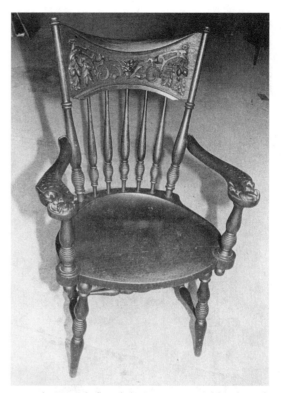

Armchair with floral design on carved back and heads impressed on arms; 25 1/2" arm to arm, 42" high. In Illinois, $425.

Ash pressed-back armchair; 23" arm to arm, 44" high. In Iowa, $165.

Armchair with pressed-design rail and splat featuring male figure with flowing mustache; 26" arm to arm, 45" high. In Illinois, $315.

→

Roman chair with grotesques on back rail; 24" arm to arm, 35" high. In Michigan, $295.

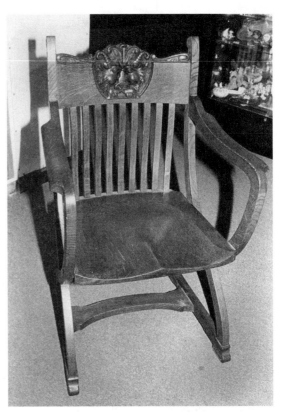

Wooden-seat armchair with grotesque design on back rail; 25" arm to arm, 39" high. In Indiana, $355.

Captain's chair or barstool that is a 1900 copy of an early-1800s style; 20" arm to arm, 30" high. In Wisconsin, $500 for a set of four.

Armchair; 24" arm to arm, 40" high. In Wisconsin, $225.

Wooden-seat double-pressed armchair with press on rail and apron; 25" arm to arm, 41" high. In Wisconsin, $265.

Deacon's chair from Illinois church; 29" arm to arm, 26" deep, 35" high. In Illinois, $245.

CHAIRS & BENCHES

Divan or loveseat with floral crest; 36" wide, 20" deep, 39" high. $495.

Loveseat with incised carving; 38" arm to arm, 23" deep, 34" high. $595.

Railroad waiting room bench with back-to-back double seat, applied flower medallion decoration above legs, and pierced designs on back and seat; 72" wide. $755.

Windsor-type bench with splayed legs and H stretcher; 39" wide, 17" deep, 36" high. $625.

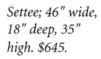

Settee; 46" wide, 18" deep, 35" high. $645.

Bench with bentwood frame, embossed, angel-like creatures on back, and two horns and faces (which cannot be seen) on seat. In Iowa, $850.

CHAIRS & BENCHES

Elm rocking bench with bent-wood arms; 44" wide, 36" high. In Illinois, $645.

Two church pews with applied decorations and impressed design on ends; 48" wide, 20" deep, 40" high. In Iowa, $375 each.

Mission-style shoeshine bench; 65" wide, 21" deep, 48" high. In Iowa, $445.

Church pew; 52" wide, 19" deep, 35" high. In Iowa, $345.

Upholstered sofa with tufted back; 44" arm to arm, 21" deep, 32 1/2" high. In Illinois. $445.

Church pew with oak sides and back, and an elm seat; 50" wide, 33" high. in Illinois, $385.

Bench; 24" wide, 14" deep, 20" high. In Wisconsin, $185.

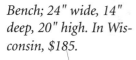

CHAIRS & BENCHES

Oak Jacobean revival-style chair, late 1870s, with Flemish spiral or twist turnings and a carved animal crest; 42 1/2" high. In Iowa, $545.

Roman chair with scooped seat; 25" arm to arm, 38" high. In Iowa, $425.

Grotesque on the rail of a chair.

←

Chair with carved tavern scene on back: 18" x 19" back, 35 1/2" high. In Illinois, $475.

Chair with upholstered seat and barrel back; 24" arm to arm, 34" high. In Michigan, $245.

Corner chair with upholstered seat; 25" arm to arm, 30 1/2" high. In Iowa, $465.

←

CHAIRS & BENCHES

Solid-seat chair, set of 6. $135 each.

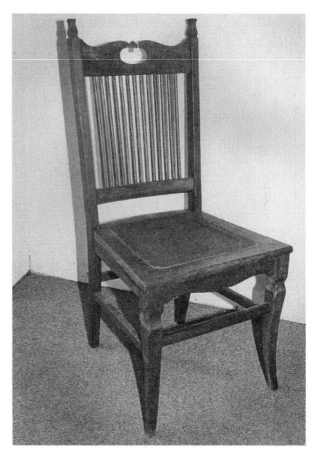

Side chair with simulated leather seat; 39 1/2" high. In Colorado, $115 each in a set of two.

Wooden-seat chair; 36" high. In Iowa, $675 for a set of eight. ←

Spindle-back chair with uphol-stered seat; 38" high. In Illinois, $395. for a set of four. →

Chapter 10

Accessories

Antique or collectible accessories – where do you put them? The answer is easy: almost anywhere. Accessories included in this chapter include both household items, and items from businesses and stores that have been adopted for home use.

In days gone by, the home sewing machine helped many a family to dress well. While the earliest sewing machine patent was issued to an Englishman in 1790, his design was not practical. Elias Howe, the man credited with inventing a workable machine, received his patent in 1846. Hand tailors and seamstresses, who felt this invention reduced their opportunities to find work, resented the use of Howe's machine. In 1854, Isaac Merrit Singer added improvements that included the foot-operated treadle. In 1889, Singer was the first to install an electric motor in a sewing machine.

Spool cabinets also make an attractive decorating accessory. Originally these cases sat on the counter at the general store, dispensing thread to lady customers. These cabinets often featured the brand name of the thread that they held – Merrick's, J. & P. Coats, and Richardson's were among the top-sellers of the day. Many versions of spool cabinets were made, ranging from those with actual desktops to those with a series of drawers with dividers. Today, spool cabinets have been employed as coffee and end tables. Smaller versions also make handy organizers for jewelry, belts, or scarves.

Items from businesses and stores have also made their way into many homes. Barber's chairs and cases are popular decorating items, as are dental cabinets. The latter usually have many drawers and doors, making them ideal organizers for small items. Old store showcases, usually with an attractive oak base and a glass top, serve as a place to display a treasured collection.

Clocks are versatile. They can be found in many parts of the home. Tall case versions stand on the floor and have become known as grandfather clocks. Others are designed to hang on walls or to sit on shelves. Mantel is a common name for a shelf clock.

Old-time clocks add interest to home decors. It is said that a clock must be perfectly level or it won't run. Because of this, some intelligent person decided to put a level in a shelf upon which the clock sat. If you have a wall clock, it is a good idea to pencil mark its best operating position on the wall so that if it is jarred in dusting, it can be returned to its correct place.

The term regulator clock was applied to any wall clock that kept accurate time. Many such clocks were made in Connecticut, a state renowned for creating timepieces. Although there were several thousand clock makers throughout the nation, Connecticut was the leader, and firms operating there took pride in the clocks they manufactured.

In this country, until about 1812, clocks were mainly found in public buildings, while in general, homes used sundials to indicate time. Primarily, through the work of one man, Eli Terry, inexpensive clocks became affordable to the masses. His competitors doubted that he would be able to produce such clocks. They knew Eli Terry had a contract to make 4,000 clocks in three years that would sell for $4.00 apiece.

This was outlandish in a day when every clock was individually made to order by hand. For Terry's purpose, crafted brass parts were too expensive. In 1807, he created machines and tools to produce identical wooden parts. He established an assembly line so each worker put in one of the interchangeable pieces. By introducing mass production to the industry, Terry actually completed 4,000 clocks that were affordable to the general public. He made a shelf type that peddlers on horse or mule back could transport with ease. Clockmakers had saved weight and space by selling the clock works only, and the purchaser was responsible for creating a case. If a case was not made and the buyer hung up the clock face and pendulum, it formed a version dubbed a "Wag on the Wall" clock. Other members of Terry's family joined the firm and operated it throughout the 1800s.

Dating of Terry's clocks is possible by looking up the various company names that changed as the partnership switched. For a quick method, in 1831 the post office address was Terrysville, in honor of Eli Junior. In 1872, the "s" was deleted to make Terryville. An Eli Terry clock would be pre-1872 if it read Terrysville, and later if the "s" is missing.

Seth Thomas was a carpenter who began working for Eli Terry in 1808, and later became a partner in the firm. In 1818, he bought a Terry patent and set up a shop of his own at Plymouth Hollow. His name became as tightly affixed to clocks of the era as the paper labels glued inside their backs. These labels listed the manufacturer, offered care and operating instructions, and presumably helped keep the clock dust-free. The town was named Thomaston in 1866 in his honor, so clocks bearing Plymouth Hollow labels precede that date.

From the inception of its clock factory in about 1802, Waterbury, Connecticut grew to become the brass and copper work center of the world. Around 1839, brass parts could be stamped out, so inexpensive metal parts became a reality, and the wooden operating clocks became passé.

In 1850, near Derby, Connecticut, Anson Phelps, an importer of tin, copper and brass, founded the Ansonia Clock Company. Late in the 1870s, the shop was moved to New York where it functioned until Russia bought its machinery in 1930.

Other Connecticut makers included the New Haven Clock Company, and William E. Gilbert's Company at Winsted. The Ingraham Company in Bristol, established by Elias Ingraham (1805-1885), created cases with classical designs that often included pillars.

Care Tips for Clock Owners

- Retain labels.

- Remove the pendulum when moving a clock so parts in it do not get bent.

- Remove the weights when moving a weight clock.

- Some clocks wind to the right; some wind to the left.

- The length of the pendulum determines the speed of the clock. Lower the bob on the pendulum and the clock will run slower. Raise it for faster movement. Remember the slogan: Lower slower, higher sprier.

- Clock repair dates are often written on the back of clocks.

Singer sewing machine that has been electrified and currently is in use; 36" wide, 17" deep, 31" high. $155.

Oak sewing cabinet with panels constructed of quarter-sawn oak showing its characteristic medullary or pith rays, which appear as vivid flakes, is enhanced by twisted pilasters, beading, and applied decorations; 24 1/2" wide, 20" deep, 31" high. In Illinois, $255.

Sewing cabinet with applied molding, decorations, and a lift-lid to pull up the machine head: 24" wide, 22" deep, 34" high, $350.

Sewing machine cabinet; 24" wide, 18" deep, 31" high. In Illinois, $225.

Sewing machine cabinet; 24" wide, 16 1/2" deep, 30 1/4" high. In Iowa, $225.

ACCESSORIES

Singer sewing machine; 36" wide, 18" deep, $155.

Sewing machine with beading and pressed designs made by Wheeler & Wilson Mfg. Co., Bridgeport, Conn., patented March 25, 1890; 33" wide, 16" deep, $155.

Singer sewing machine; 35" wide, 17" deep, 30 1/2" high. In Illinois, $155.

ACCESSORIES

Sewing machine cabinet; 32" wide, 18" deep, 31" high. In Illinois, $295.

Quarter-sawed oak sewing machine cabinet with applied decorations; 22" wide, 18" deep, 30" high. In Illinois, $275.

Singer sewing machine with carvings on doors and applied decorations; 36" wide, 18" deep, 30" high. In Iowa, $155.

Spool cabinet counter desk supplied by J. & P. Coats to storekeepers as an advertising promotion. Store accounts were kept inside the lift-lid section; 30" wide, 21" deep, 12" high, $545.

Richardson's spool cabinet with ten glass-front drawers and one made of wood; 20" square, 25" high, $745.

Label found on the back of the Richardson's spool cabinet.

Merrick's spool cabinet with a brass date plaque marked "July 20, 1897." Spools of thread were inserted through a covered hole in the top into the circular spool holder and when the holder was rotated by the knob at the top, the appropriate spool could be positioned for removal through the base door; 18" diameter, 20" high, $950.

Corticelli Silk and Twist spool cabinet with 26 glass-front drawers and 4 wooden drawers; 45" wide, 18" deep, 43" high, $1,550.

J. & P. Coats spool cabinet counter desk resting on a metal sewing machine stand to form a self-standing desk; 30" wide, 21" deep, 12" high, $525.

Label found on the back of the counter desk.

Merrick's Six Cord Cotton spool cabinet dated July 20, 1897, with two revolving spool dispensers flanking the mirror (the thread weights range from 8 to 100); 31 1/2" wide, 17 1/4" deep, 23 1/2" high. In Illinois, $1,250.

Spool cabinet; 24" wide, 16 1/2" deep, 17 1/2" high. In Iowa, $615.

Crowley's needle cabinet; 19" wide, 9 1/2" deep, 9 1/2" high. In Iowa, $375.

Store-counter desk and spool cabinet with lift-lid top; 30" wide, 22" deep, 17" high in back. In Wisconsin, $525.

ACCESSORIES

Store-counter desk and spool cabinet with lift-lid top; 33" wide, 23" deep, 15" high. In Illinois, $525.

J. & P. Coats spool cabinet; 21" wide, 15" deep, 8" high. In Illinois, $295.

One-half section of a Corticelli double-spool cabinet with one side replaced; 23" wide, 17" deep, 32" high. In Iowa, $625.

ACCESSORIES

Type cabinet manufactured by the Hamilton Mfg. Co., Two Rivers, Wis., with all handles stamped "Hamilton Mfg. Co."; 37" wide, 22" deep, 43" high, $825.

Type cabinet manufactured by Hamilton Mfg. Co., Two Rivers, Wis., Los Angeles, Calif., and Rabway, NJ; 42" wide, 26" deep, 44" high, $595.

Hamilton printer's cabinet made in Two Rivers, Wisconsin; 65" wide, 24 1/2" deep, 44" high. In Georgia, $895.

Barber cabinet with two drawers, a fall-front door, and open storage space in the base; 24" wide, 14" deep, 36" high, $515.

ACCESSORIES

Barber cabinet with two swing-out doors and a fall-front door at the base; 16" wide, 9" deep, 19" high, $290.

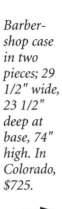

Barber-shop case in two pieces; 29 1/2" wide, 23 1/2" deep at base, 74" high. In Colorado, $725.

One section of a barber's back bar with white-marble top, two mirrors, and a cabinet that measures 24" wide, 14" deep, 39" high. There are four such sections in the total back bar with a measurement of 15'4" wide, 14" deep, 97" high. In Indiana, $6,500.

Hanging wall cabinet with drawer was a free gift from Koch if you purchased the complete barber-shop fixtures from them; 14 1/2" wide, 7" deep, 21" high. In Colorado, $325.

ACCESSORIES

Dental cabinet; 26" wide, 17" deep, 59" high, $1,150.

Dental cabinet; 29 1/2" wide, 14 1/2" deep, 60 1/2" high. In Colorado, $1,500.

Portable dental cabinet in case; 14 1/2" wide, 9 1/2" deep, 14" high. In Iowa, $345.

Dental cabinet with brass pulls; 39" wide, 15 1/2" deep, 33 1/2" high. In Ohio, $1,500.

Dental cabinet; 26" wide, 11" deep at top and 17" at base, 60" high. In Illinois, $1,150.

Dental cabinet with two rolltops, applied decorations, and brass hardware; 33 1/2" wide, 18 1/2" deep, 30" high. In Iowa, $1,950.

Machinist's chest with a label reading "Union, The Chest Co., Inc., Rochester, N.Y." currently used to store jewelry, scarves, belts, and sundries; 20" wide, 8" deep, 13" high, $255.

Watchmaker's cabinet; 20 1/2" wide, 6 1/2" deep, 12 1/2" high. In Illinois, $575.

ACCESSORIES

Hanging wall cabinet from a church; 29" wide, 7 1/2" deep, 28" high. In Iowa, $395.

Apothecary case; 24" wide, 4" deep, 24" high. In Wisconsin, $315.

ACCESSORIES

Baker's cabinet from Elmyra, New York; 50 1/2" wide, 26 1/2" deep, 28 1/2" high. In Georgia, $850.

Jeweler's desk with glass pulls; 36" wide, 20" deep, 39" high. In Illinois, $765.

Railroad desk with a slanted lift-lid top; 34" wide, 24" deep, 50" high at back, 46" high at front, $495.

Railroad map case and table base. The four pullout drawers contain maps of Tennessee, Georgia, Mississippi, and Arkansas; 29" wide, 22" deep, 31" high. In Tennessee, $375.

Store display case with two sliding doors; 34" wide, 10" deep, 34 1/2" high. In Wisconsin, $285.

Hardware store display case; 32" wide, 14" deep at bottom, 6" deep at top, 50 1/2" high. In Iowa, $350.

ACCESSORIES

Ice cream table with metal frame and claw and ball feet; 25" square, 29" high. In Iowa, $345.

Close-up of metal head on the corner of the apron on the ice cream table.
→

Brass, marble, and oak shoeshine stand from Dallas, Texas; 22" wide, 36" deep, 62" high. In Colorado, $845. Wooden barber pole from Maine; 75" high, $595. Barber sign; 18" diameter, 8" deep; $350. Three-station marble top barbershop backbar; $4750.
←

Blauls Better Brand Beans (B.B.B.B.) Coffee box with hinged dropdown lid; 24" wide, 22 1/2" deep, 32" high. In Colorado, $325.

ACCESSORIES

Store display case; 72 1/2" wide, 18 1/4" deep, 35 1/2" high. In Illinois, $1,500.

←

Showcase from early 1900s Alaskan jewelry store with ten drawers accessible in back; 72" wide, 24" deep, 41" high. In Alaska, $1,595.

→

"Time Is Money" shelf clock with thermometer and level built in; 15 1/2" wide, 5 1/2" deep, 24" high. In Colorado, $265. Oak and walnut clock shelf; 18" wide, 6 1/4" deep, 8 1/2" high, $115.

Ansonia mantel clock; 14" wide, 5" deep, 22" high, and $250. Clock shelf; 25" wide, 8" deep, 10" high, $225.

ACCESSORIES

Seth Thomas eight-day mantel clock; 15" wide, 5" deep, 23" high, $325.

Eight-day wall clock marked "Eclipse" (the model name) on back; 14" wide, 4" deep, 29" high, $325.

Ansonia wall clock; 14" wide, 5" deep, 38" high, $1,150.

Label on the back of the Ansonia wall clock showing its prize medal award at the Paris Exposition in 1878.

ACCESSORIES

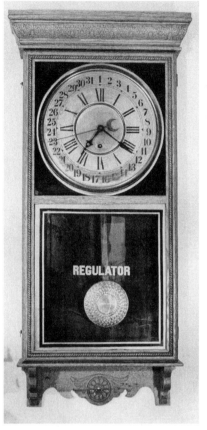

Waterbury regulator calendar wall clock; 16" wide, 5" deep, 34" high, $645.

Waterbury regulator clock; 16" wide, 4 1/2" deep, 37" high. In Iowa, $525.

Ingraham shelf clock with label on reverse that reads, "The Lilac, The E. Ingraham Company, May, 1917"; 15" wide, 21" high. In Alaska, $295.

ACCESSORIES

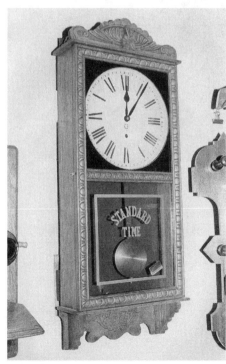

Wall clock; 15" wide, 5" deep, 32" high. In Wisconsin, $495.

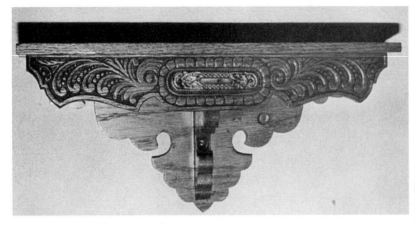

Clock shelf with built-in level; 14 1/2" wide, 4 1/4" deep, 6 1/4" high. In Illinois, $215.

←

Tampa calendar clock made by the New Haven Clock Co.; 14" wide, 4 1/2" deep, 22" high. In Iowa, $495.

Ansonia shelf clock with pressed designs on case; 15" wide, 23" high. In Alaska, $395.

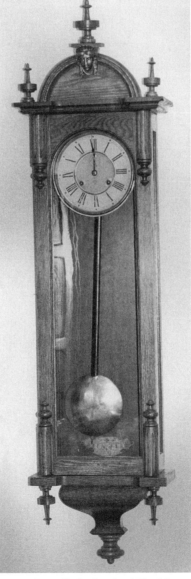

Ansonia wall clock; 13 1/2" wide, 6 1/2" deep, 55" high. In Iowa, $875.

ACCESSORIES

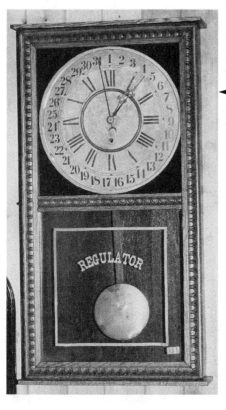

Gilbert calendar wall or shelf clock; 14" wide, 4" deep, 28 1/2" high. In Iowa, $675.

Ingraham wall or shelf clock; 15" wide, 4 1/4" deep, 29" high. In Ohio, $675.

Waterbury wall clock with brass weights; 14" wide, 5" deep, 36" high. In Iowa, $1,650.

Gilbert shelf clock; 17" wide, 4" deep, 24 1/4" high. In Iowa, $395.

ACCESSORIES

Wall clock; 14 1/2" wide, 4" deep, 36" high. In Iowa, $545.

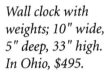

Wall clock with weights; 10" wide, 5" deep, 33" high. In Ohio, $495.

Octagonal school-type wall clock; 17" wide, at face, 3 1/2" deep, 30" high. In Pennsylvania, $525.

Octagonal school-type wall clock; 18" wide, at face, 3 1/2" deep, 32" high. In Ohio, $495.

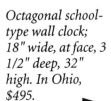

Time clock manufactured in Endicott, New York, by International Time Recording, which today is IBM; 13 1/2" wide, 10" deep, 40" high. In Iowa, $650.

Time clock manufactured by the Cincinnati Time Recording Co., Cincinnati, Ohio; 13 1/2" wide, 7" deep, 35" high. In Illinois, $565.

Ansonia schoolhouse clock manufactured by the Ansonia Clock Co., New York, Circa 1878; 13" wide, 20" high. In Kentucky, $355.

Gilbert time and strike mantel or shelf clock with pressed design on case surround; 15" wide, 5" deep, 22" high. In Illinois, $275.

ACCESSORIES

Ansonia octagonal school-type clock; 11" wide at base, 18" wide at top, 32" high. In Wisconsin, $550.

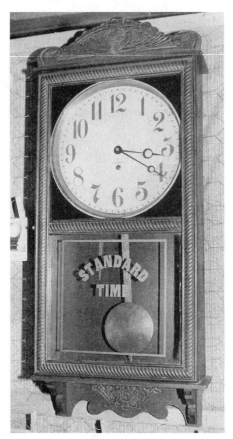

Regulator clock 16" wide, 5" deep, 32" high. In Kentucky, $515.

Octagonal school-type clock; 12" wide, 4" deep, 23" high. In Tennessee, $495.

Ingraham shelf clock; 15" wide, 5" deep, 22" high. In Wisconsin, $295.

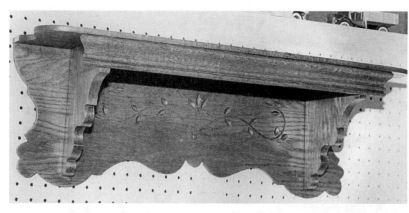

Clock shelf with spoon-carved garlands; 27" wide, 9" deep, 9" high. In Illinois, $195.

Clock shelf- 24" wide, 8" deep, 8" high. In Iowa, $195.

Ingraham shelf clock; 15" wide, 5" deep, 23" high. In Wisconsin, $295.

Shelf clock; 13" wide, 5" deep, 23" high. In Iowa, $295.

ACCESSORIES

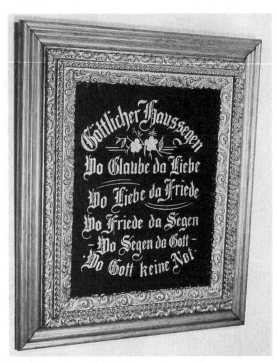

Frame with gold leaf liner surrounding German religious motto, 18" wide, 21" high, $165.

Frame with a decorative gold trim outline around picture and on the outer edge; 17" wide, 20" high, $195.

Multilinear frame; 28" wide, 32" high, $165.

Mirror with gold leaf liner and oak outer surround, 27" wide, 30" deep, $185.

ACCESSORIES

Double-framed mirror, 29" wide, 51" high, $215.

Framed mirror, manufactured by LifeTime Furniture, Grand Rapids, Bookcase & Chair Co., Hastings, Michigan; 18" wide, 32" high, $245.

Wall mirror; 22" wide, 45 1/2" high. In Ohio, $265.

Multilinear framed mirror; 27" wide, 29" high. In Illinois, $165.

*Frame with gold inner and outer outline; 22"
diameter. In Illinois, $155.*

*Multilinear gilt frame on oak easel; 29 1/2" x 33 1/2".
In Illinois, $215 for easel, $245 for framed picture.*

ACCESSORIES

*Multilinear oak gilt frame;
24" x 27". In Illinois, $185.*

→

Frame with gilt inner lining holding Paul Norton print of Prospect Park, Moline, Illinois; 25" x 21". In Illinois, $245.

Quarter-sawed-oak beveled wall mirror with applied decorations; 27" wide, 23" high. In Iowa, $195.

Multilinear framed mirror; 27" wide, 29" high. In Illinois, $175.

What-not stand with artificially grained shelf supports and ladder-back to imitate bamboo; 16" wide, 12" deep, 37" high, $245.

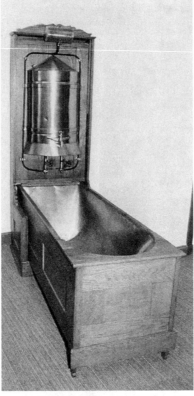

Copper-lined folding bathtub with a copper water reservoir; 27" wide, 65" in length, 73" high, $3,500.

Bookshelf with three slatted shelves; 20" wide, 13" deep, 38" high, $155.

Built-in bookcase, one of the features of the early bungalows; 35 1/2" wide, 42 1/2" high. In Illinois, $425.

Game table, late 1880s, with cabriole legs and concave bottom shelf that allows for legroom. The removed top shows spinning pointers for a game; 32" square, 29" high, $695.

Pool ball rack; 23 1/2" wide, 4 1/4" deep, 19 1/2" high. In Wisconsin, $225.

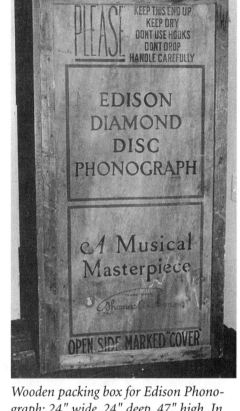

Wooden packing box for Edison Phonograph; 24" wide, 24" deep, 47" high. In Wisconsin, $100. Also seen in Illinois, $400.

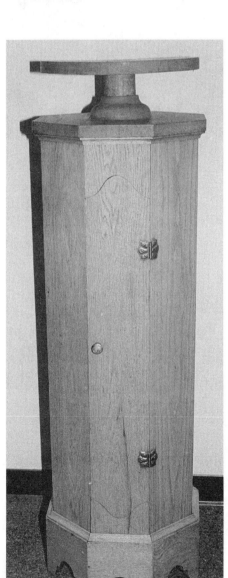

Octagonal cellarette (liquor cabinet) with revolving top and single front door; 17" wide, 54" high. In Alaska, $395.

Liquor cabinet with scroll feet and a door with shelves for holding bottles; 20" wide, 16" deep, 34" high, $295.

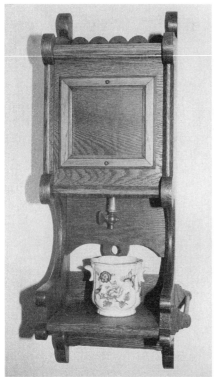

Hanging water fountain from a Mississippi riverboat has a towel-bar side. Behind the framed glass on the face was placed the scheduled stops along the Mississippi; 11" wide, 9" deep, 28" high. In Colorado, $450.

←

Easel with oil landscape; 27" wide, 99" high. In Kentucky, easel $275; landscape $350.

Fireplace mantel with beveled mirror, applied decorations, incised carvings, and four pillars supporting the cornice; 62" wide, 103" high. In Indiana, $2,150.

Fire screen with needlepoint picture; 23" wide, 26" high. In Iowa, $175.

Fireplace mantel with applied decorations on posts and below shelf; 60" wide, 82" high. In Iowa, $945. ◀

Smoking stand with metal striker and replaced ashtray; 9" square, 27" high. In Illinois, $125. ▶

Fireplace mantel with applied carving and green tiles framing hearth opening; 60" wide, 12" deep, 46" high. In Indiana, $1,200. ◀

Shoe store footstool with twisted metal legs; 10" wide, 25" long, 14" high. In Illinois, $125. ▶

ACCESSORIES

Bobsled; 45" long, 16" wide, 12" high. In Tennessee, $295.

Tobacco truck used in warehouse to carry two baskets of tobacco, 38" square by 5" deep. Truck measures 85" wide, 35" deep, 22" high. In Tennessee, $345.

This label found on an oak wardrobe advertises Shallene Bros., dealers in furniture in Moline, IL. Saving labels can preserve valuable historical and geographical information about the furniture you find.

Trunk or tool chest with brass handles; 27" wide, 18" deep, 13" high. In Illinois, $295.

Fretwork from an old home. In Colorado, $425.

ACCESSORIES

Chapter 11

The Arts and Crafts Movement

Ruskin, Eastlake, Morris, Stickley, Hubbard – rebels one and all. With harsh, swift hands these men, who emphasized craftsmanship, brushed away shoddy machine-work, and late Victorian clutter, curves, and eclecticism. Quiet, peaceful and practical designs would prevail at home, according to their philosophy.

This was not a newborn concept. In the late 1700s, England's architect brothers, Robert and James Adam, promoted a beautiful, but sterile, union of architecture and furnishing in which everything was compatible. Even mirrors and wall hangings had assigned stations in the elegant design, and were to remain there permanently. Consoles and statues were given permanent niches. Floors reflected the same swags and medallion motifs as the ceiling above. Perfection and coordination became the pattern of the era.

In the latter half of the 1800s, another group accepted this idea of oneness. Men who followed this cult challenged the establishment. John Ruskin, for one, believed all work should pass three tests. Is it honest, useful, and cheerful? William Morris, another thinker of the movement, stated that "Real art is the expression by man of his pleasure in labor." They believed that only the useful and beautiful should be in a home, and neither price nor fashion should determine art or quality. A dedication to hand workmanship was sought by members of the British Art Workers Guild. Interior designs, glass, jewelry, printing, ceramics, architecture, and furniture were all influenced by this new expression. To the promoters, individual achievement in the craft was essential, even if its results were quaint and crude. They ignored the fact that machines made many products available to the rising middle-class purchaser that formerly only the wealthy could afford. The movement's detractors realized that machines could not be turned off quickly. They were needed and could not be disregarded. The movement was not greeted with delight by the masses.

Was it a London-born reformer, writer, art critic, and Oxford professor who was the granddaddy of the English Arts and Crafts Movement which spread to continental Europe as well as, in some degree, to the United States? This man, affluent John Ruskin (1819-1900), at least deserves a portion of the credit. Perhaps because he was acquainted with Biblical teaching, he supported social reforms and spent much of his inheritance improving the conditions of the working class.

Ruskin felt that good architecture was related to moral feelings and, therefore, was religious in tone. Some authorities think Ruskin's discussions did help foster change.

Another rebel felt that cheap and slipshod work often resulted from the rapid machines, but he was not opposed to their contributions and use. Straight is strong. Simple is striking. Box it up. These were three concepts advocated by England's Charles Locke Eastlake (1836-1906). He might well have believed in the geometric principle that the shortest distance between two points is a straight line, for he maintained that round designs wasted wood. His book, *Hints on Household Taste*, published in 1868, promoted designs with rectangles and squares. Chip carving and incised parallel lines, sometimes referred to as railroad tracks, were attractive decorative touches that did not recklessly use extra wood. Eastlake opposed the marketing of inferior commercial wares that were turned out too rapidly by some factories. His mass-production-oriented predecessors and contemporaries were apparently so delighted with the ability of their power driven machines that they borrowed, adopted, and combined any patterns from the past that pleased them. Eastlake found this eclectic tendency disturbing. His uncluttered designs crossed the Atlantic and settled in the United States around 1870, retaining their hold on fashion until about 1890. While Eastlake and his devotees in England tended to use oak or ash, walnut was still the number one wood in America, although it was waning both in popularity and availability.

Eastlake's rectilinear plans were accepted by the furniture industry. Designers were hired to "go" creative, and what some of them did to his box-like designs was disturbing. So many appendages and doodads were added that the resulting products did not have the simple look advocated by Eastlake. He liked the clean, practical, functional Japanese furniture, or the touches of steeples and tracery borrowed from old Gothic designs. Although it was difficult to discard all the frills immediately, the industry was ready for a change and wanted to promote plainer styles. Thus, England's Charles Locke Eastlake did foster a new trend where curves where out of style and going straight was fashionable.

Another leader of the English Arts and Crafts Movement, poet William Morris (1834-1896), was an interior designer who advocated the return to excellence in total craftsmanship. Since he delved into church history as a college student, it was fitting that he helped establish a company that specialized in ecclesiastical furnishings. Wood carvings, embroidery, tapestries, stained-glass windows, murals, and mosaics were produced, until, as the business expanded, it served secular interests as well. Wallpaper, furniture, and carpets all received Morris' attention. However, this poet is probably most commonly associated with the invention of the Morris chair – the chair which permitted reclining. The upholstered back could be slanted at various angles. A movable rod in the back of the chair, placed in the desired groove, retained the proper incline for one's comfort.

The next cultural revolutionary, Gustav Stickley (1857-1942), is credited with developing a new style of furniture, indigenous to the United States. Its lines remind one of Morris's functional recliner with its uncluttered look. Perhaps Stickley was under William Morris's sphere of influence.

Who was Gustav Stickley? If you had asked him, he would have told you he was the creator of THE UNIQUE Craftsman furniture. All other staunch, straight-lined, strong oak examples were copies that could not compare, he would have said. He disliked imitations and was not flattered that furniture makers emulated his work. This multifaceted man was a writer, designer, manufacturer, editor, and homebuilder who developed squat bungalow houses which contrasted with the tall, wood-wasting edifices that surrounded them. These smaller homes were inexpensive and provided the "just right" setting for his Stickley's Craftsman furnishings. Coordination of exterior and interior designs was a key theme of the Arts and Crafts Movement. With the passage of years, the Stickley-copyrighted Craftsman name was swallowed up by another title which distressed and disturbed this builder. The generic term used by competitors who fashioned their furniture after his was "Mission," the name currently assigned to this style.

Another dissident in the United States was Elbert Hubbard (1856-1915), who led his army of dissenters to establish a craft colony at East Aurora, New York. Just as Brigham Young guided the Mormans westward to settle, irrigate, and reclaim the dry wasteland in Utah, Hubbard inspired and nourished handmade artistry in a mechanized wasteland.

This peaceful revolutionary worked for a time with his brother-in-law, John D. Larkin. The latter started a company using his name in 1875. By 1892, the company became the Larkin Soap Manufacturing Company. Hubbard was a published writer and a skilled advertising agent who helped develop the "Larkin Club" for housewives and their friends and relatives. Housewives were encouraged to join the Larkin Club, earning delightful premiums in exchange for purchases. Years after Hubbard's demise, these groups remained in existence. The free 1925 fiftieth anniversary catalog listed Larkin's alluring array of household products. Free gifts, available as awards for promoting Larkin Clubs, included "Furniture, lamps, rugs, curtains, silverware, linens, and other lovely things for the home." Buffalo, New York, was the manufacturing location for Larkin furniture.

Elbert Hubbard left his brother-in-law's company after he visited England and accepted William Morris's rejection of machines. By 1895, handicraft artisans who joined Hubbard's East Aurora Colony became known as "Roycrofters," and their products are usually marked "Roycroft." They created pottery, leather articles, textiles, jewelry, metal objects, in addition to printing books. Their straight-lined, handmade furniture was in the Mission style, adapted from that designed by Gustav Stickley.

On May 7, 1915, a newspaper headline read, "Passenger Ship Lusitania Sunk by German Sub. 1,198 perish, including 128 Americans." Among those lost was Elbert Hubbard. The Roycrofters had lost their leader.

These are only a few of the men who influenced the Arts and Crafts Movement. Many architects, artisans, builders, artists, and designers rejected overmechanization, finding it distasteful, and turned to the wholesome nourishment of creative hand craftmanship.

Parlor table with Eastlake influence, as seen by the incised designs; 32" wide, 22" deep, 28" high, $395.

Fall-front Eastlake parlor desk with incised lines and carving; 29" wide, 16" deep, 60" high, $945.

Parlor table with the incised lines characteristic of Eastlake; 30" wide, 21 1/2" deep, 30" high. In Iowa, $345.

Eastlake fall-front secretary, circa 1880; 39" wide, 11" deep at top, 18" deep at base, 91" high. In Michigan, $1,595.

ARTS & CRAFTS

Eastlake cane chair with incised designs and lines, set of 4, $325.

Eastlake side chair with tufted velvet back, applied designs on uprights, and incised lines; 39" high, $195.

Cane seat chair with an incised bird and flower design in the back rail, an example of Eastlake's rectangular, plain lines; 34" high. In Colorado, $165.

Close-up of the incised design in the back rail of the Eastlake chair.

Morris chair with retractable footrest and adjustable height rod in back; 29" arm to arm, 40" high. In Alaska, $595.

→

Morris-type upholstered armchair with rolled arms and grotesques on leg uprights; 28" arm to arm, 39" high, $445.

Morris chair with pullout footrest and pressed carving; 30 1/2" arm to arm, 39" high. Not oak. In Iowa, $465.

→

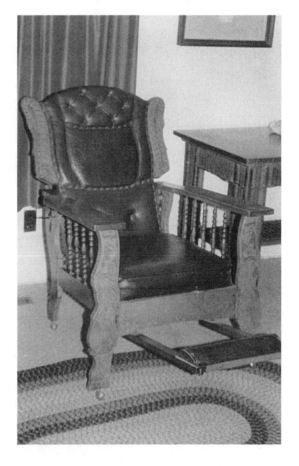

ARTS & CRAFTS

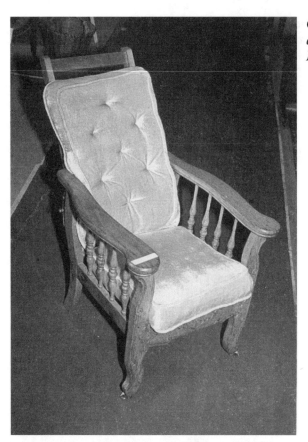

Child's Morris chair with rod at back for adjusting slant; 19" arm to arm, 27" high. In Michigan, $365.

←

Morris-style recliner chair; 31" arm to arm, 35" high. In Kentucky, $345.

Child's Morris chair with paw feet; 21" arm to arm, 27" high. In Illinois, $345.

←

Morris chair with scooped apron design and incised decorations on legs; 27" arm to arm, 42" high. In Illinois, $355.

→

Seen from left to right: AJ. M. Young, New York, quarter-sawed oak Morris-type chair featuring side slats to the base stretcher, corbels on arms, through- or exposed arm tenons, and a wooden bar at the back to adjust reclining position; 31" arm to arm, 37" deep, 36" high; $1,450. Quarter-sawed round oak lamp table, possible handcrafted as it hasn't been found in catalogs; 24" diameter, 28" high; $350. Mission-style wooden table lamp with a slag glass shade; 16" square, 23" high; $425. Unknown maker mission rocker with slats under arms, front arm corbels and exposed arm tenons; 32" arm to arm, 29" deep, 36" high; $875.

Morris chair with incised carving on front legs and apron and grotesques on arm ends; 30" arm to arm, 31" high. In Alaska, $695.

→

ARTS & CRAFTS

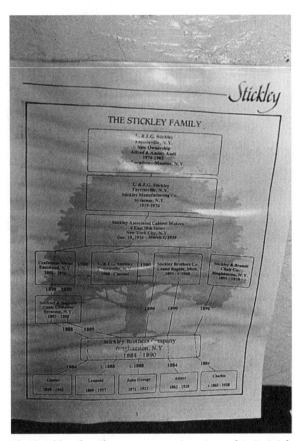

The Stickley family tree as seen in a L. and J.G. Stickley Co., Fayetteville, N.Y., catalog. This company is currently manufacturing the best examples of old mission furniture.

Oval folding parlor table with spool legs and a label underneath reading, "Quaint Furniture, Stickley Bros. Co., Grand Rapids, Mich."; 24" wide, 19" deep, 24" high. $485

The label found underneath the oval folding table.

ARTS & CRAFTS

Sewing rocker with a metal label reading "Quaint Furniture, Stickley Bros., Grand Rapids, Mich."; 31" high, $295. ➤

Standing ashtray stand made by Stickley Bros., Grand Rapids, Michigan; 10" diameter, 30" high. In Illinois, $245.

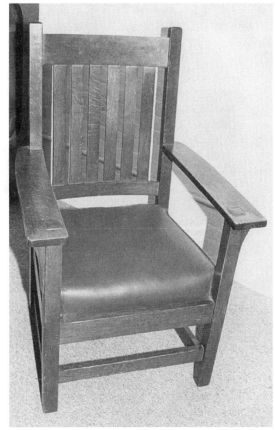

Armchair in original finish with exposed arm tenons, corbels, pegs, and a paper label reading "Quaint Furniture, Stickley Bros."; 27" arm to arm, 40" high, $325. ➤

The decal and the burnt-in labels found on the Quaint table from South Dakota.

Stickley Brothers #2570 Quaint table; 40" wide, 26" deep, 30" high. In South Dakota, $595.

Stickley Brothers #3752 Quaint youth or day bed. In Iowa, $850.

ARTS & CRAFTS

"Quaint Furniture," Stickley Bros. Co., Grand Rapids, Michigan, original finish round lamp table with leg tenons through the top; 24" diameter, 30" high; $795. Table lamp with copper and slag glass shade; 18" square, 24" high; $925. L. and J.G. Stickley quarter-sawed oak slatted armchair with pegs, through-arm tenons and a beveled front seat rail (an L. and J.G. Stickley design); 28" arm to arm, 26" deep, 38" high; $950. The pieces on the back shelves are examples of Arts and Crafts candlesticks and pottery by Roseville, Weller, Van Briggle, McCoy, Teco, Fulper, and Marblehead. →

"Quaint Furniture," Stickley Bros. Co. desk; 36" wide, 23" deep, 36" high. A two-piece set with matching armchair that is not shown is $995. ←

"Quaint Furniture," Stickley Bros. Co. settle that can be found in one of their catalogs; 62" wide, 26" deep, 37" high, $1,050. ←

The mark, used from 1910 to 1912, that was found on the L & J.G. Stickley table from Iowa.

L & J.G. Stickley #530 Handcraft one-drawer table; 48" wide, 30" deep, 30" high. In Iowa, $695.

ARTS & CRAFTS

Rocker with corbels, pegs, new leather cushion, and replaced rockers with a red Gustav Stickley decal inside back stretcher; 25" arm to arm, 36" high, $425.

Gustav Stickley chair with slat back and rush seat; 36" high, $1,500 for set of 6.

Mission oak, rush seated occasional or side chair with exposed pegs. Also available with a leather, slip seat. The trademark Als ik kan (Dutch motto meaning "As I Can") surrounded by an old joiner's compass and Gustav Stickley's signature are stamped in now-faded red on the back upright post. 36" high. In Illinois, $315.

Gustav Stickley's "Als ik kan" decal.

ARTS & CRAFTS

Bookcase with arched apron, a style used by Harvey Ellis, who worked for Stickley from 1903 to 1904; 48" wide, 12" deep, 51" high. In Virginia, $895.

Gustav Stickley #815 two-door china cabinet (painted blue inside) showing Harvey Ellis's influence with sloping top rail and arches at base; 39" wide, 15" deep, 64" high. In the Midwest, $4,950.

Gustav Stickley #225 even-arm settle without the spring-cushion seat; 78" wide, 31" deep, 29" high. In Minnesota, $6,500.

Gustav Stickley #354A V-back arm-chair, 26" arm to arm, 36" high; #354 V-back side chair, 36" high. In Missouri, a set of two arm chairs and four side chairs, $3,500.

Unmarked arm rocker with hard leather seat and an outline where the tag was; 26" arm to arm, 39" high. Gustav Stickley #305 1/2 sewing rocker with leather seat and burnt-in joiner's mark; 17" wide, 31" high. In Iowa, arm rocker $250 and sewing rocker $675.

Gustav Stickley dining room table and chairs; table 48" x 63", 30" high; master or host chair, 20" arm to arm, 38" high; side chairs, 34" high. In Nebraska, the nine-piece set including table, 6 chairs, a sideboard and a china cabinet, $9,500.

ARTS & CRAFTS

Gustav Stickley #636 Ellis-inspired game table with arched apron and stretchers; 48" diameter, 30" high. In Minnesota, $1,200.

Gustav Stickley library table with corbels on legs, pegged construction, through-leg tenons and hammered copper drawer pulls, $975.

Gustav Stickley #656 split-pedestal table that extends to 12 feet has a large red decal label; 54" diameter, 29" high. #370 ladder-back chairs that have small red decal labels; 36" high. #814 1/2 sideboard with ooze leather in the top drawer and a burnt-in mark on the drawer's side; 56" wide, 21" deep, 48" high. In Minnesota, table $2,250; ladder-back chairs $1,200 for six; sideboard, $1,500.

ARTS & CRAFTS

Gustav Stickley #212 V-back settle made between 1907 and 1912 with original hard leather seat and both the red decal and paper label; 47" arm to arm, 24" deep, 36" high. In Ohio, $2,750.

Gustav Stickley #922 full-sized bed with both paper and black burnt labels; 59" wide, headboard 55" high, footboard 46" high. In Nebraska, $5,750.

Gustav Stickley #369 bent-arm reclining chair with original laced-leather seat; 33" arm to arm, 38" deep, 41" high. In Missouri, $5,275.

Gustav Stickley sewing chair (referred to as Thornden rocker) in dark fumed oak with rush seat, circa 1901; 31" high. In Illinois, $575.

Library table that has a lift-up writing desk and inkwell when the drawer is fully opened. A manufacturer identification inside the drawer reads "Limbert Arts & Crafts Furniture Co."; 42" wide, 28" deep, 30" high, $695.

Mission chair marked "Limbert" under left arm with exposed arm tenons and pegs; 24" arm to arm, 39" high, set of 6, $1,700.

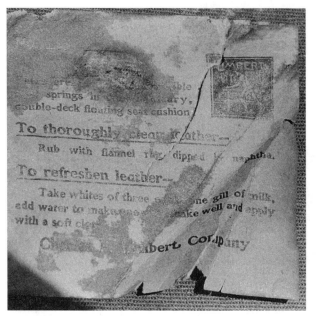

Mission oak arm rocker made by Limbert Arts Crafts Furniture of Grand Rapids and Holland, Michigan; 27 1/4" arm to arm, 33 1/2" high. In Wisconsin, $425.

A Limbert label found at the bottom of a chair's seat cushion.

ARTS & CRAFTS

Unmarked Gustav Stickley-style rocker on the left with a replaced leather seat; 28" arm to arm, 34" high. Limbert rocker on the right with branded mark under the arm; 27" arm to arm, 32" high. In South Dakota, unmarked Stickley style $425 and Limbert $450.

The burned-in-trademark found in the top-drawer of the Limbert chest.

Limbert chest of drawers with elaborately carved drawer fronts; 36" wide, 20" deep, 45" high. In Michigan, $875.

Limbert rocker with brown leather seat and added upholstery pad on the back; 27" arm to arm, 33" high. In Iowa, $495.

An example of the mark used by the Roycrofters.

Roycroft original finish fall-front desk with name impressed on gallery; 43" wide, 19" deep, 58" high, including buyer's premium, $7,150.

The Roycroft cross and orb symbol.

Arts and Crafts Movement cupboard attributed to Roycroft by its owner; 36" wide, 12" deep, 85 1/2" high. In Ohio, $1,450.

ARTS & CRAFTS

The Roycroft symbol found on the base of a brass jardiniere.

Roycroft chair with an impressed cross and orb trademark symbol in the center of the front apron; 40" high, $545.

Roycroft book-stand with 14 volumes of Little Journeys by Elbert Hubbard, Copyright 1916 by Roycrofters. Keyed tenon construction and marked Roycroft on a diamond-shaped metal tag on the side of the shoefoot; 26" wide, 14" deep, 26" high. In Iowa, $455.

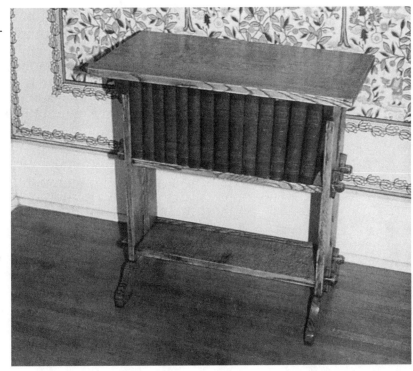

ARTS & CRAFTS

Larkin chiffonier that has an "information" label on the back; 33 1/2" wide, 17 1/2" deep, 47 1/2" high. In Iowa, $555.

Larkin chiffonier that has a "perfect condition" label on the back (see text); 34" wide, 18" deep, 47 1/2" high. In Illinois, $585.

Larkin china cabinet; 34" wide, 15" deep, 56" high. In Colorado, $795.

Larkin sewing desk with folding legs and top; 48" wide, 24" deep, 26" high. In Iowa, $345.

ARTS & CRAFTS

Chapter 12

Mission Furniture

There are conflicting reports as to how the native-to-America Mission furniture was conceived. Was it a derivative of the English Arts and Crafts Movement, or was it religious in origin? Some say its roots are in the crude, straight-lined furnishings pounded together out of necessity by long-robed Spanish monks and their converted Indian parishioners, who struggled to construct utilitarian seats and tables for their rustic churches in the old Southwest. This appealing tale would explain both the name and the austerity of the Mission style. As if to prove their religious ancestry, some chairs and benches have cut out crosses on their backs.

The 1908 Sears, Roebuck and Company catalog displays a banner presenting "Special Values in Mission Furniture." It enthusiastically proclaims that the style is not an experiment but, after years of availability, retains its popularity. Prominent architects recommended the furnishings to clients since they blend strength, comfort, beauty, and simplicity. The ad links secular commercialism with the religious by explaining that similar furnishings were found in Spanish missions in the Southwest, and designs based on their structure received the approval of the Arts and Crafts Society in both England and the United States.

Other authorities feel the name has a different origin. Furnishings have a purpose or mission. A bed is for resting. A chair is for sitting. A table is to sit at or to hold items. Each piece had its own reason for being. Another explanation comes from George Grotz who writes with mirth and meaning in his informative books. He contends that Gustav Stickley wanted to coordinate architecture and furniture. In order to accomplish this unification, Stickley developed stoic craftsman furnishings to compliment the bungalows he designed and constructed. A promoter called these structures Spanish mission and the name stuck, not only to the walls of the abodes but to the contents inside as well. Perhaps a combination of these different theories explains Mission oak with its strength and strict, simple lines.

But who could explain Gustav Stickley? The man was an enigma. He renounced the furniture produced by his emulators in his magazine, "The Craftsman," and also in his catalogs. Stickley crossed off his copiers – Hand-Craft, Mission, Roycroft, Quaint, Arts and Crafts, and others. What hurt him the most, however, was that his family members produced wares under the name "Stickley Furniture."

Why buy the shadow when the genuine article was available? He contended that Craftsman was the best. But here's the puzzlement. Gustav Stickley did not do what another designer did. John Belter (1795-1865) laminated rich woods, such as rosewood, walnut, and oak, and then tortured, bent, and pierced them, ornately carving natural motifs. It is said that this 19th century craftsman destroyed his designs to frustrate and deter copiers. Stickley, on the other hand, believed in home do-it yourself projects. He encouraged amateurs to send for his designs so that they, too, could build quality furnishings inexpensively at home. His materials were available to those who sought to be creative. Customers could order leather, upholstery material, metal trim, and plans with instructions. Fabrics, which were stamped for needlework, intrigued the ladies. Stickley felt that pleasing, well-designed, well-executed furniture helped improve the moral fiber of a home. He did not like the senseless, overly ornate furniture cherished by John Belter and his peers. Sincere furnishings helped shape honest men and women, according to Stickley's philosophy. Despite the fact that loss of sales might hurt him financially, he spread the tenet of hand-made furniture. The Arts and Crafts Movement influenced Gustav Stickley when he visited England and Europe, and he adopted some of their teachings. His attitude was: Commercial imitators – no! Home handymen – yes!

Early in his life, this Wisconsin farm lad worked in furniture factories and stores learning about wood, construction, styles, and merchandising. This exposure fostered his dislike for the flimsy, fussy furnishings mass-produced in factories. In spite of his dislike, Stickley and his four brothers manufactured conventional, late Victorian furniture from about 1880 to mid-1890. The Stickley Brothers Company is mentioned in material at the Grand Rapids Public Library. A leaflet, "Furniture - the Product of Pride," stated that from 1880 to 1900 more than 85 furniture manufacturers started business in that city, including the Stickley Company.

Gustav Stickley wanted to improve the quality of furniture while reducing its cost. He opened a workshop in Eastwood, near Syracuse, New York, around 1895. By 1898 he was experimenting with plain, functional, solid, comfortable, durable, rectangular lines as his Craftsman ideas took their natal step. Stickley did not plan to develop a new furniture design. It just happened. His baby, Craftsman, became an integral part of his life, and he adopted almost a perfectionist attitude in his desire to create each piece well. Purchasers were encouraged to return any unsatisfactory pieces so quality could be retained. His wood specialty was white oak, but he also used other indigenous varieties.

Wood requires a coating of some type to prevent shrinking and swelling in humidity, and to keep it from absorbing dirt or acquiring stains. A sealing agent also helps accentuate the character and beauty of the lumber used. Various finishes are applied to furniture. Stickley liked fumed oak because it resembled patina, the natural darkening of furniture with age, use, and exposure to light. To obtain this appearance, Craftsman articles were moistened to open the pores and placed in an airtight compartment, usually for forty-eight hours, depending on the depth of color desired. Containers of strong ammonia provided the vapors that penetrated the wood, which later was meticulously hand-sanded until smooth. Stickley applied his own special coating to achieve one of three tones – a soft silver gray, or a light or deep brown. Craftsman wood-luster was rubbed on to complete the process, making his fumed oak furniture ready for marketing.

Although purists usually want pieces left as found to preserve their value, some owners do not like this finish and have found it difficult to remove. One man exclaimed, "After I stripped the surface, I sanded for days and finally got it clean. It was a devil of a job!" Gustav Stickley was so proud of his workmanship that such treatment of one of his wooden offspring might have made him angrily grit his teeth, but it was his own belief that furnishings should fit the home and provide comfort for the owners. If they said, "Let it be light," that would be their choice. However, an owner should think twice before changing the finish, because many collectors would embrace the original fume finish ecstatically.

Seat cushions were covered with genuine leather or sheepskin specially treated not to craze, and waterproofed to add endurance. Cheaper versions manufactured by other firms were made of artificial leather, but these were not fine enough to pass Stickley's standard for softness and beauty.

By 1900, Stickley sought to share his bold, utilitarian lines with the world. He displayed samples of his original design at the Furniture Exposition in Grand Rapids, Michigan. Visitors realized that Gustav Stickley had introduced a new, uncluttered furniture style. Others seized upon his ideas and, with a few changes in design and titles, presented similar furniture.

Keeping it all in the family, Gustav Stickley's younger brothers Leopold and J. George brought him the greatest anguish by copying his designs. The brothers were capable of developing quality products of their own, and their imprint, "The work of L. and J. G. Stickley," indicated outstanding workmanship. Located in Fayetteville, they worked near their brother's Eastwood location.

Disturbed by the proliferation of idea-snatchers, Stickley marked his pieces three times. One unique device he used was a joiner's compass of ancient vintage. Joiners pre-dated cabinetmakers. In the days before glue and metal fasteners, such as nails and screws, these workers joined pieces of wood together to form furniture. They depended on wood pegs (dowels), wedges or special joints such as the mortise and tenon (which Stickley faked) to unite the parts. Between the prongs of his patented red joiners compass, Stickley inserted a Dutch motto that read: "Als ik K" which means "As I Can." Beneath this stamp he placed his first and last name. The Craftsman label comprised the other registered marking which was meant to protect the rights of both the designer and the purchaser. By the time his 1913 catalog was published, Stickley modestly declared that most of his furniture "was so carefully designed and well-proportioned…that even with my advanced experience I cannot improve upon it." His competitors helped drive him into bankruptcy in 1916. He lived to see his furniture go out of style a few years later. His words were prophetic when he declared that his furniture would be worth many times its original cost in fifty or one hundred years. Its scarcity and quality would make it so. An under fifty-dollars chest of drawers with Stickley's three marks might bring several thousand dollars today. As the originator of an American style, he has been vindicated for his belief in austere furniture. How disturbing it must have been when his quality Craftsman furniture was lumped together with all other grades of functional oak furniture under the generic heading, " Mission."

Other makers continued to produce Mission-style furniture, but its popularity was waning by the 1920s. The Come-Pact Furniture Company of Toledo, Ohio advertised a Morris-look chair for $8.75 plus a library table for $11.75. Their quarter-sawed white oak had a good appearance in any of its eight finishes.

The Mother's Home Life magazine for February 1925 contained an inviting advertisement. To those who would hurry to order the pictured, six-piece fumed oak set, a seven-piece genuine cut-glass water pitcher with tumblers would be sent as a free bonus. The demand for Mission furniture was decreasing rapidly, and a new buying trend could be seen when installment buying was introduced. Housewives could go into debt for household furnishing with one dollar down and three dollars monthly with a full year to pay. Another era was beginning, and credit merchandising was emerging.

Stickley Brothers arm rocker made by Quaint Furniture, Grand Rapids, Michigan; 25 1/2" arm to arm, 32" high. In Iowa, $465.

←

Close-up of brass plate found on mission rocker.

Mission-style bench; 46" wide, 23" deep, 39" high. In Michigan, $495.

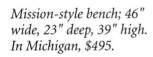

→

Mission-style youth rocker. The name Stickley Brothers, Grand Rapids, Michigan, is burned into the underside of the seat. 31" high. In Illinois, $295.

←

Mission-style rocker with label reading, "Quaint Furniture, Stickley Bros. Co., Grand Rapids, Michigan"; 28" arm to arm, 39" high. In Illinois, $395.

→

Mission bench once used as a shoe-shine stand in a barbershop; 62" arm to arm, 38" high. $795.

→

The interior section of a fall-front Stickley Brothers mission desk made by Quaint Furniture of Grand Rapids, Michigan; 34 1/2" wide, 17 1/2" deep, 45" high. In Wisconsin, $745.

Mission-style teacart with black stamp on bottom reading, "Stickley Bros., Co., Grand Rapids" 17" wide, 28" long, 29" high. In Alaska, $545.

Mission arm-chair with uphol-stered seat; 26" arm to arm, 37" high. $295.

Harden quarter-sawed oak mission rocker with curved arms, long side slats, through tenons on front of box, and through-arm tenons; 30" arm to arm, 36" high, $845.

Ecclesiastical bench with crosses in back splats and arm uprights; 46" arm to arm, 42" high. $695.

Mission rocker with uphol-stered seat; 27" arm to arm, 32" high. $225.

Mission-style sofa bed; 61" wide, 34" deep, 38" high. In Alaska, $1,195.

MISSION FURNITURE

Child's mission-style chair; 29" high. In Illinois, $165.

Child's mission-style rocker; 17 1/2" arm to arm, 28" high. In Iowa, $225.

Mission oak hall tree showing the flakes of quarter-sawed oak; 26 1/2" wide, 19" deep, 76" high. In Iowa, $895.

Mission-style chair table in table position; 27" wide, 35" deep, 30" high.

Mission-style chair table with cushion seat and back. See following picture for table position. In Illinois, $595.

MISSION FURNITURE

Mission oak sewing rocker with leather seat and pullout compartment for sewing supplies; 32" high. In Illinois, $245.

Mission oak armchair; 25" arm to arm, 36" high. In Illinois, $265.

→

Mission oak hall tree made of quarter-sawed oak with metal hooks and lift-lid storage compartment; 31" wide, 17 1/2" deep, 82" high. In Iowa, $995.

←

Mission oak lift-lid necessary chair, also called commode or potty-chair; 24 1/2" arm to arm, 35" high. In Illinois, $225.

Mission-style child's rocker; 17" arm to arm, 23" high. In Iowa, $245.

→

Mission-style sewing rocker with pull-out drawer on side; 35" high. In Michigan, $215.

Rocker with Mission feel; 23" arm to arm, 34" high. In Illinois, $245.

Mission-style youth rocker; 17" arm to arm, 32" high. In Iowa, $245.

Mission oak footstool with upholstered top; 18 1/2" wide, 14" deep, 16 1/2" high. In Iowa, $245.

Footstool in the mission oak style; 15 1/2" wide, 12" deep, 10" high. In Illinois, $225.

Mission library table with a single drawer that opens in the front and back; 42" wide, 26" deep, 31" high. $595.

Mission library table; 42" wide, 26" deep, 31" high. $595.

Mission oak library desk; 49" wide, 30 1/2" deep, 30" high. In Wisconsin, $475.

Mission-style library table with one drawer; 48" wide, 30" deep, 30" high. In Alaska, $725.

Mission oak stand; 15" square, 28 1/4" high. In Wisconsin, $295.

Mission smoking stand; 12" wide, 11" deep, 30" high. $295.

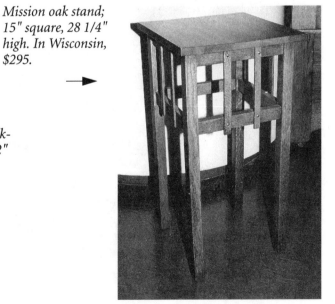

Mission fall-front desk with a label reading "Western Cabinet Co., Burlington, Ia."; 28" wide, 14" deep, 62" high. $945.

Mission-style fall-front parlor desk; 28" wide, 17" deep, 40" high. In Michigan, $525.

Combination Mission-style bookcase-desk with fall-front desk in center; 63" wide, 17" deep, 51" high. In Michigan. $975.

←

MISSION FURNITURE

Fall-front mission oak desk; 29 1/2" wide, 15 1/2" deep, 60" high. In Iowa, $1,250.

Mission oak fall-front desk; 31 1/4" wide, 17 1/2" deep, 46 1/2" high. In Iowa, $595.

Mission-style fall-front desk; 36" wide, 14" deep, 42" high. In Iowa, $745.

Mission oak bookcase with mullions on doors, mortise and tenon construction on bottom and top of stiles, and the arched apron, characteristic of Harvey Ellis; 46 1/2" wide, 13" deep, 50 1/2" high. In Wisconsin, $815.

MISSION FURNITURE

Built-in cabinet taken from a home designed in mission style; 32" wide, 15" deep, 57 1/2" high. In Iowa, $495.

Bookcase with arched apron, similar to the type that Ellis used on Gustav Stickley furniture. In Wisconsin, $945.

Quarter-sawed oak mission china cabinet with muntins on doors and side panels; 38" wide, 16" deep, 57" high; $795.

Mission oak clock; 10 1/2" wide, 4 1/2" deep, 16 1/4" high. In Iowa, $255.

Mission oak clock; 14" wide, 6" deep, 31 1/2" high. In Iowa, $365.

Mission clock with brass pendulum and weights; 20" wide, 17" deep, 77" high. $2,495.

Mission oak clock; 12" wide, 5" deep, 25" high. In Iowa, $245.

Mission-style chifforobe; 40" wide, 18" deep, 64" high. In Michigan, $595.

MISSION FURNITURE

Lamp; 17" square shade, 27" high. In Wisconsin, $395.

Mission-style server; 42" wide, 18" deep, 50" high. In Iowa, $465.

Mission-style oak buffet; 55" wide, 18" deep, 51" high. $495.

Mission oak server or buffet with a fumed finish; 40" wide, 20" deep, 37 1/4 high, 8 1/2" rail. In Iowa, $465.

Mission doll's bed; 13" wide, 22" deep, 11" high. $185.

Mission-style sewing machine made by Free Sewing Machine Co., Rockford, Ill. Patented May 20, 1913; 25" wide, 18" deep, 31" high. In Michigan, $345.

Mission oak utility cabinet with spade feet; 20" wide, 15 1/2" deep, 43 1/2" high. In Illinois, $350.

Umbrella stand with mission lines; 9" x 9 1/2", 26 1/2" high. In Iowa, $185.

Smoking stand with mission style; 13" square, 28" high. In Illinois, $245.

Mission oak smoking stand with slagtype green-and-white glass in door; 17 1/2" wide, 11 1/4" square top, 28" high. In Illinois, $245.

MISSION FURNITURE

Glossary

American Windsor Chair a graceful chair of the 1700s with many slender spindles in its back. *Splayed* (slanted out) legs went into the seat, which was generally scooped out to resemble a saddle. Customarily, no apron was present. The so-called oak captain's chair or barstool of the early 1900s is a debased Windsor.

Annual rings a tree's concentric seasonal growth layers inside the tree trunk. These bull's-eye like circles can easily be seen on a stump of the base of a log where it is severed from the tree.

Applied decoration an ornamentation crafted separately and applied to a piece of furniture.

Architectural antiques include items such as fireplace mantels and barber's back bars. These items were built-in structures in homes and businesses.

Artificial graining a technique that uses paint or stain to imitate the grain of a specific wood. In the early 20th century, many catalogs referred to this as "antique oak" finish.

Atlantes a male image that often functions as a supporting column on furniture.

Baker's cabinet a cabinet that evolved from a table that had such features as a bin for flour, provisions for pans, pull-out boards for kneading and cutting, perhaps a divided bin for meal and sugar, and drawers for cutlery and linen.

Beading a type of molding with raised shapes that resemble beads.

Bed lounge resembles a couch with a back added. In addition, it opens to provide a sleeping surface.

Bentwood a style of chair made from curved, bent wood, it was created by Austrian Michael Thonet about 1840.

Bombay front or sides swell or bulge out. They are convex.

Bookcase-desk a combination of two pieces of furniture – a bookcase and a desk. Today these units are often referred to as *secretaries* or *side-by-sides*. Usually the desk is on the right but there are some made for left handed people with the desk on the left.

Buffet a piece of furniture with drawers and cupboards for dishes, table linens, silver, and other dining needs. Another term for this storage unit is *sideboard*.

Cabriole leg a leg with a double curve flowing out at the knee, in at the ankle, then slightly outward again.

Cane a long, narrow strip of rattan used for weaving chair seats and backs. Cane chairs can be woven by hand with strands of rattan woven through holes that surround the seat frame. When grooves encircling the chair seat are present, prewoven sheets of cane are forced into them and glued tightly in place with a spleen cover. This forms a pressed cane seat.

Cheval mirror a large, swinging looking-glass mounted on a frame. It usually stands on the floor so that a viewer is able to see a full-length reflection. The cheval dresser received its name because it includes a tall swinging mirror that was supported in a frame.

Chiffonier a tall chest of drawers. Currently, many people refer to them as *highboys*.

Chifforobe a piece of bedroom furniture made with a chest of drawers on one side and a narrow wardrobe on the other.

Chimera a fire-breathing creature from Greek mythology with a lion's head, a goat's body, and a serpent's tail. Generally, a horrible creature of the imagination.

China buffet a cross between a sideboard and a china cabinet, embodying the characteristics of each.

Claw foot a furniture foot carved to resemble the claw of a bird.

Close grained means that pores are difficult to observe. In some species, you may even require the help of a magnifying glass to detect the pore's presence.

Closed cupboard or blind cupboard has solid wooden doors.

Commode an enclosed, cupboard-type washstand, usually including one or more drawers or door.

Cornice a horizontal molding found on the top of furniture pieces.

Cylinder a curved, sliding top on a desk or secretary. Also, a desk or secretary with a rounded front.

Deck a small-encased drawer mounted on the tops of a dresser. Today they are generally called *handkerchief boxes*.

Diner a late-1800s or early-1900s catalog name for a dining room chair. Nonetheless, the term dining room chair appeared simultaneously.

Divan a couch or sofa.

Draw table a rectangular table with a double top. The lower level is divided so that it can be drawn out and pulled up at each end to add to the table's length. Many of these are English imports. Also called a *refectory table*.

Dressing table and bench became important around 1920 when many women began to use makeup. It was convenient to have a place to keep their cosmetics and to sit before a mirror while they were applying makeup. Also called a *vanity table*.

Drop lid or front a hinged lid on a desk that drops down to form a writing surface.

Eclectic adapting and combining designs and styles of various periods.

Eight-day clock a clock that only needs to be wound once a week, rather than daily.

Extension table a table top that pulls apart so leaves may be added to enlarge it.

Fainting couch is the present day term for an elongated, backless seat with a rolled pillow at one end. Here it was possible for a person to sit or lie down. Old catalogs refer to it as a couch.

Fall-front another term for a hinged lid on a desk that drops down to form a writing surface.

Finial a carved, cast, or turned terminal ornament on furniture, clocks, and accessory pieces.

Fingerhold a cutout part in a chair's back rail.

Flakes the large, pronounced pith rays characteristic of oak.

Fretwork an ornamental border perforated or cut in low relief.

Gesso with a plaster of Paris base can be carved, gilted, or painted for use as raised decorations on furniture.

Grain the arrangement and direction of fibers in wood that give the different species of wood their characteristic textures, markings, and patterns.

Grotesque a figure or part of a figure of an animal or person, often mixed with flowers, fruits or foliage in an unnatural way.

Handkerchief box a small, encased drawer attached to a dresser top. Also referred to as a *deck*.

Highboy a word in current use to refer to a chiffonier.

Hoosier cabinet generic name for a kitchen cabinet with a pullout work surface, flour bins, drawers, sifters, cupboard space, etc. This one-unit cabinet was made in the late 1800s and early 1900s in the Hoosier state (Indiana) and elsewhere. Different companies used other names for the cupboard.

Icebox referred to as a refrigerator in old catalogs. Because they are in great demand, they are currently being made.

Incised a design cut into the surface of the wood.

Lady's desk one of the many terms used to refer to a small parlor desk.

Lamp table a small table designed to hold a kerosene lamp or candles. After homes were electrified, the new electric lamps were also placed on these tables.

Library table a table to hold books, periodicals, and newspapers. Library tables often had a drawer and a shelf underneath.

Marriage pieces of furniture combined as one when they were not originally a single unit. An example would be a bookcase top added to a drop-front desk to form a secretary.

Medullary ray (see pith ray)

Molding a shaped strip of wood used for ornamental purposes.

Morris chair a reclining chair with an adjustable rod which enabled the sitter to change the degree of incline. Named for its designer, poet William Morris.

Mortise and tenon the mortise is a slot or hole in a piece of wood. A tenon is a protruding tongue or prong in another piece of wood that fits snugly into the mortise to form a tight joint. They may be pegged where they join.

Ogee a molding with a continuous double curve.

Open cupboard may have doors with glass panes or may have no doors at all.

Open grained refers to woods that have pores that are easily visible. Open grained woods accept stains readily.

Parlor desk a small desk, usually found in a living room or parlor. Also called a lady's desk or a fancy desk.

Patented furniture includes highchairs that convert to rockers or go-carts. Patented platform rockers of different types offer secure seats for those who distrust the tilting and creeping characteristic of ordinary rockers.

Paw feet furniture feet that resemble an animal's paws.

Pedestal table a popular dining room table with a pedestal base, sometimes the base will be made of a double pedestal. These tables were usually extension tables, which could be expanded with the addition of leaves.

Pediment a horizontal decorative feature mounted on the top of a tall piece of furniture. It is often curved in a scroll or arched shape.

Pie safe with punched tin panels or screens was a storage unit for baked goods. It allowed air circulation and kept the rodents and flies away from the food.

Pilaster an artificial decorative pillar with no structural strength that is set against a background. Frequently, it is half-round or rectangular.

Plain-sawn (plain-sawed) indicates that boards are cut from the whole log, lengthwise in parallel sections at right angles to the rays. On oak, a pattern of stripes and elliptical Vs result.

Platform rocker a chair that moves back and forth on an elevated frame, rather than on curved rockers. Orignally called a patent rocker.

Pores small openings for the discharge and absorption of fluids.

Quarter-sawn (quarter-sawed) the log was cut in half lengthwise. Each half was then cut in half again. This cutting formed four equal rounded-end triangles (pie-shaped wedges), that were sliced parallel to the rays and across the growth rings.

Refectory table a rectangular table with a double top. The lower level is divided so that it can be drawn out and pulled up at each end to add to the table's length. Many of these are English imports. Also called a *draw table*.

Regulator clock the name given to any wall clock that kept accurate time.

Roll-top a flexible hood that slides down as a rounded lid on a desk, made of narrow, parallel, wooden slats glued to a flexible base of duck or linen in the same fashion as tambour doors were made.

Rung a crosspiece that connects cabinet, chair, or table legs at the bottom (also called stretcher or runner).

Secretary a desk – usually with a bookcase above, and a series of drawers below the writing surface.

Sectional bookcase abounded in the early 1900s. Each glass-enclosed unit could be purchased separately and fit into place one above the other. Bases and tops were available to complete these cases.

Serpentine a snakelike curve on the fronts of furniture.

Sideboard (see buffet)

Side-by-side another term for a bookcase-desk combination.

Slant-front the hinged drop lid on a desk or secretary that provides a writing surface when opened.

Slat horizontal crossbar in chair backs.

Splat the center upright in a chair back.

Splay slant out, especially chair legs that slant from the seat to the floor.

Spoon carving decorative carving that resembles the bowl of a spoon.

Step-back a cupboard with a top that sits slightly back on its base and is smaller in depth than its base.

Stile the vertical piece in a frame or panel of furniture.

Straight front a cupboard that has a continuous straight-up-and-down line.

Stretcher (see rung)

Swell-front an old catalog term synonymous with the word convex.

Taboret a small plant stand.

Tambour a door made of wooden slats glued on a duck or canvas backing that operates either vertically or horizontally in a groove.

Tavern table is constructed so that the top remains uncluttered for card playing. Underneath the top and usually at each corner are compartments where participants can keep their beverages or snacks.

T-back a modern term for chairs with backs that resemble a printed capital T in configuration.

Tilt-top table a small table, usually found in a parlor or living room, whose top can be tilted so that it is perpendicular to the floor.

Turning shaping wood with chisels on a lathe to form table and chair legs or other items.

Vanity table (see dressing table)

Veneer a thin layer of decorative wood glued over the surface of a cheaper wood.

Wardrobe a piece of furniture in which garments were hung and stored before closets were a common feature in the home.

Bibliography

Books

Aronson, Joseph. *Encyclopedia of Furniture.* New York: Crown Publishers, Inc., 1965.

Ayars, Marcy and Walter. *Larkin Oak.* Summerdale: Echo Publishing, 1984.

Brown, Don. *Oak Furniture Styles and Prices.* Des Moines: Wallace-Homestead Book Co., 1975.

Cathers, David M. *Furniture of the American Arts and Crafts Movement: Stickley and Roycroft Mission Oak.* New York: New American Library, 1981.

Cole, Ann Kilborn, *How to Collect the New Antiques.* New York: David McKay Company, Inc., 1966.

Durant, Mary. *The American Heritage Guide to Antiques.* American Heritage Publishing Co., Inc., 1970

Grotz, George. *The New Antiques.* Garden City, New York: Doubleday & Company, Inc., 1964.

Hamilton, Charles F. *Roycroft Collectibles.* London: The Tantivy Press, 1980.

Hill, Conover. *Antique Oak Furniture.* Paducah: Collector Books, 1976.

Mackay, James. *Turn of the Century Antiques.* New York: E.P. Dutton & Co., Inc. 1974.

Miller, Robert W. *Clock Guide Identification with Prices.* Des Moines, Iowa: Wallace-Homestead Book Co., 1974.

Ransom, Frank Edward. *The City Built on Wood, a History of the Furniture Industry in Grand Rapids, Michigan.* Ann Arbor, Michigan: Edards Bros.,Inc.,1955.

Stickley, Gustav and L. and J.G. Stickley. Stickley Craftsman Furniture Catalogs: *Craftsman Furniture Made by Gustav Stickley* and *The Work of L. & J.G. Stickley.* Introduction by David Cathers. New York: Dover Publications, Inc., 1979.

Swedberg, Robert W. and Harriett. American Oak Furniture Styles and Prices, Book I, third edition. Radnor PA: Wallace-Homestead Book Co., 1992.

——. *American Oak Furniture Styles and Prices, Book II,* second edition, Radnor, PA: Wallace-Homestead Book Co., 1991.

——. *American Oak Furniture Styles and Prices, Book III,* second edition. Radnor, PA: Wallace Homestead Book Co., 1988.

Catalogs

Chittenden & Eastman Company Furniture Distributors. *Catalogs.* Burlington, Iowa: Chittenden & Eastman Company, 1892 through 1950.

Israel, Fred L., ed. *1897 Sears, Roebuck Catalogue.* New York: Chelsea House Publishers, 1976.

Life-Time Furniture, The Cloister Styles. Reprinted from original catalog. New York: Turn of the Century Editions, 1981.

Limbert Furniture. Reprinted from original catalog. New York: Turn of the Century Editions, 1981.

Mirken, Alan, ed. *1927 Sears, Roebuck Catalogue.* New York: Bounty Books div., Crown Publishers, Inc., 1970.

Montgomery Ward & Co., Catalog No. 99. Chicago, fall and winter 1923-24.

Montgomery Ward & Co., Catalog No. 110. Chicago, spring and summer 1929.

Sears, Roebuck and Co. Catalog No. 154. Chicago, spring and summer 1927.

Schroeder, Joseph J., Jr., ed. *Sears, Roebuck & Co. 1908 Catalogue No. 117.* Chicago: The Gun Digest Company, 1969.

Shop of the Crafters at Cincinnati Furniture Catalog. New York: Turn of the Century Editions, 1983.

Ward's Catalog for Spring and Summer No. 118. Chicago: 1933.

Periodicals

Koehler, Arthur. *The Identification of Furniture Woods, Circular No. 66.* Washington: United States Department of Agriculture, November 1926.

Index

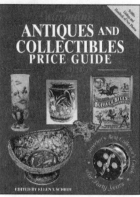